T0339474

Cambridge Elements ≡

Elements in Politics and Society in Latin America
edited by
Maria Victoria Murillo
Columbia University
Juan Pablo Luna
The Pontifical Catholic University of Chile
Tulia G. Falleti
University of Pennsylvania
Andrew Schrank
Brown University

THE POLITICS OF LGBTQ RIGHTS EXPANSION IN LATIN AMERICA AND THE CARIBBEAN

Javier Corrales
Amherst College

CAMBRIDGE
UNIVERSITY PRESS

CAMBRIDGE
UNIVERSITY PRESS

University Printing House, Cambridge CB2 8BS, United Kingdom

One Liberty Plaza, 20th Floor, New York, NY 10006, USA

477 Williamstown Road, Port Melbourne, VIC 3207, Australia

314–321, 3rd Floor, Plot 3, Splendor Forum, Jasola District Centre, New Delhi – 110025, India

103 Penang Road, #05–06/07, Visioncrest Commercial, Singapore 238467

Cambridge University Press is part of the University of Cambridge.

It furthers the University's mission by disseminating knowledge in the pursuit of education, learning, and research at the highest international levels of excellence.

www.cambridge.org
Information on this title: www.cambridge.org/9781108995207
DOI: 10.1017/9781108993609

First published 2021

A catalogue record for this publication is available from the British Library.

ISBN 978-1-108-99520-7 Paperback
ISSN 2515-5253 (online)
ISSN 2515-5245 (print)

The Politics of LGBTQ Rights Expansion in Latin America and the Caribbean

Elements in Politics and Society in Latin America

DOI: 10.1017/9781108993609
First published online: November 2021

Javier Corrales
Amherst College

Author for correspondence: Javier Corrales, jcorrales@amherst.edu

Abstract: The first section of this Element reviews the history of LGBTQ rights in the region since the 1960s. The second section reviews explanations for the expansion of rights and setbacks, especially since the mid 2000s. Explanations are organized according to three themes: (1) the (re-)emergence of a religious cleavage; (2) the role of political institutions such as presidential leadership, political parties, federalism, courts, and transnational forces; and (3) the role of social movement strategies, and especially, unity. The last section compares the progress on LGBTQ rights (significant) with reproductive rights (insignificant). This Element concludes with an overview of the causes and possible future direction of the current backlash against LGBTQ rights.

Keywords: LGBTQ rights, abortion, religion, Catholics, Evangelicals, secularism, machismo, feminism, trans-feminism, AIDS, homophobia, transphobia, hate crimes, public opinion, same-sex marriage, tolerance

ISBNs: 9781108995207 (PB), 9781108993609 (OC)
ISSNs: 2515-5253 (online), 2515-5245 (print)

Contents

Introduction

One of the most important breakthroughs in contemporary democratic theory is the proposition that true democracy requires equal treatment – by states and citizens – of people whose sexual orientation and gender identity defy hetero- and cis-normative standards.[1] The notion that homophobia and transphobia are not just social ills, but also democratic deficiencies is one of the most transformative ideas of the late twentieth century (Rahman 2000, Weiss and Bosia 2013).[2] It is based on the idea that the right to liberty, equality, and dignity also requires the right to sexuality (Rios 2018). The purpose of this Element is to summarize the scholarly literature documenting the evolution of this idea in Latin America and the Caribbean since the 1960s.

I will organize my thoughts by focusing on the specific political challenges faced by individuals and movements defending the rights of lesbians, gays, bisexuals, transgender, and queer people (LGBTQ), the latter consisting of all people defying hetero- and cis-normative standards. Thematically, I organize these challenges in terms of cultural attitudes and ideologies, political institutions, and internal characteristics of the social movements advocating for LGBTQ rights and pro-LGBTQ policies. Chronologically, I organize challenges by historical periods: the authoritarian era of the 1960s to late 1970s, the democratization era of the 1980s and 1990s, the rights-expansion era of the 2000s, and the current backlash era. For each of these historical periods, I discuss both challenges and achievements in implementing LGBTQ rights and policies.

An important theme in this review is that challenges and achievements have varied across different periods and countries, so much in fact, that it is difficult to find a common thread for the whole region. That said, one feature that has been constant in the fight for LGBTQ rights in Latin America is confrontation with religious actors, traditionally the Roman Catholic Church, but increasingly Evangelical churches. This does not mean that religious groups are the only actors that pose resistance; secular groups on both the left and the right have been strong blockers at different points in history. Nor does it mean that religious groups are always unsupportive; progressive Christianity in the region may be weaker now than in the past, but it is still influential and often sympathetic to LGBTQ causes. However, it does mean that the resistance

---

[1] Cis is a Latin-origin prefix used to denote the opposite of trans. Cis refers to "this side of," whereas trans refers to "on the other side of." When applied to sexuality and gender identity, cis refers to people who adopt a gender identity that matches the sex assignment made at birth, often based on genitalia characteristics. See Aultman (2014).

[2] Although calls from scientists and humanists to decriminalize sodomy in the West date back to the nineteenth century, the struggle to equate sexuality rights to human rights is a mostly late-twentieth-century phenomenon (see Symons and Altman 2015).

coming from religious groups has been consistent and open throughout this period and has even intensified more recently.

Studying LGBTQ rights is therefore not just about changing norms, mobilizing society, revamping institutions, and building transnational networks – all standard building blocks of the struggle for democracy – but, increasingly, also about fighting organized Christianity. This is no small struggle. The Catholic Church is one of the most ancient, powerful, and enduring forces in the West, dating back to Roman times. While Catholicism in Latin America has never been monolithic or even monopolistic, the Catholic clergy remains strongly influential and increasingly socially conservative (Hagopian 2008). Adding to their power, Evangelical actors have joined forces with the Catholic clergy behind its socially conservative agenda (Boas 2021), making religious resistance even more powerful than in previous decades.

Because of this clash with conservatism and, more specifically, with organized Christianity, the story of LGBTQ politics in Latin America and the Caribbean has all the elements of the proverbial David and Goliath analogy: a small movement of marginalized minorities challenging a vast force representing large majorities and counting on important allies, a young movement confronting a long-established network, an underdog taking on a giant. Seen from this perspective, the achievements of the LGBTQ movement are nothing short of extraordinary. One way that this Element demonstrates this point is by comparing the LGBTQ movement's achievements with a parallel struggle: abortion rights. Except in Cuba, Uruguay, Argentina, and Mexico, the region remains fairly prohibitionist over abortion rights, a clear sign of the enduring power of conservatism.

So how has the LGBTQ movement been able to overcome conservative and religious resistance? An equally important theme in this Element is to review interactions between pro-LGBTQ social movements and other actors or political institutions. Some of these interactions have been posited to help overcome conservative resistance. The literature agrees that the rise of an *organized* and *relatively united* pro-LGBTQ social movement is the sine qua non for headway. But it is insufficient. Movements need to form ties with other political actors or interact with institutions. The challenge is to figure out what type of interactions and which allied actors/institutions are more likely to help LGBTQ movements change the status quo.

Scholars have offered hypotheses about a variety of potential allies, such as: (1) larger and more institutionalized social movements (e.g., feminists, human rights activists), (2) parts of the bureaucracy (e.g., health ministries, ombudsman), (3) political parties (typically on the left), (4) subnational institutions (especially in federal systems), and (5) courts (domestic and international). This review will show that each of these interactions carries potential for overcoming resistance, but only under certain conditions, and in some cases, some of these interactions can also carry risks that can in the end hinder progress.

This Element concludes with a brief view of future challenges. Despite LGBTQ achievements, the Goliath in this story is not defeated. The conservative forces continue to demonstrate ability to fight back and often prevail, and this is one way in which the story of LGBTQ rights in Latin America departs from the David and Goliath analogy.

1 What the LGBTQ Movement Is up Against

Scholars studying LGBTQ rights tend to agree that the politics of expanding LGBTQ rights is an uphill battle, to say the least. Socioeconomic and institutional hurdles are onerous: the LGBTQ community is small everywhere (representing a tiny fraction of the politically active population), often able to hide (i.e., staying in the closet), frequently short of economic resources and political allies, and subject to animosity from conservative religion (Badgett et al. 2014).

In Latin America, one could argue these hurdles are accentuated in relation to advanced economies of the West: resistance to identifying openly as LGBTQ is strong, very few celebrities and political leaders are out, LGBTQ individuals still find living in the closet more acceptable than LGBTQ individuals in more secular societies, income levels are lower, philanthropic organizations willing to help LGBTQ groups are far more limited, and conservative religion combined with machismo is particularly strong (Corrales and Pecheny 2010, Pecheny 2010, Encarnación 2011, 2015, Díez 2015, Domínguez-Ruvalcaba 2016, Reynolds 2020). And given the region's serious governance problems, LGBTQ issues must compete against what many people in the electorate would deem to be higher development priorities, such as fighting poverty, inequality, economic distortions, corruption, crime, authoritarianism, climate change, education deficits, etc.

In addition, scholars have always emphasized a feature inimical to LGBTQ tolerance that is especially salient in Latin America: strong intersectionalities of discrimination (Domínguez-Ruvalcaba 2016). In most Latin American countries, the groups that are most highly discriminated against – non-whites and the poor – are often majorities. Many LGBTQ people in Latin America have identities that intersect with these two categories. Thus, the average LGBTQ person in Latin America is likely to face not just homo- and transphobia, but also racism and aporophobia.[3] In the 1980s and 1990s, during the height of the

---

[3] Aporophobia is a type of classism. The latter refers to any type of class-based discrimination intended to privilege one class (typically an upper class) relative to others. Aporophobia refers to a specific form of fear, mistrust, and exclusion of the poor. It may be experienced by people of any class, not just the upper class. See Bustos Rubio and Benito Sánchez (2020).

AIDS crisis, another important category of intersectional discrimination was health related, with LGBTQ people often stigmatized by their health status or health risks. And more recently, with the expansion of refugee populations in many Latin American countries and the rise of nativism, LGBTQ expatriates often suffer the added discrimination of xenophobia.

That fact that LGBTQ identities in Latin America intersect so widely with other marginalized cohorts is important because, as we will see, many of the gains achieved by the LGBTQ community have to do with rights, and rights in Latin America are significantly less palpable in marginalized communities (McGee and Kampwirth 2015). For a white, upper-class gay man in Rio de Janeiro, the achievements of LGBTQ rights movements in their country mean far more than say the same rights would for a black gay man living in a favela (Mascarenhas Neto and Zanoli 2019). Those rights are even less palpable if the subject is lesbian, trans, a sex worker, or a refugee.

Understanding intersectionalities is also important because they can exacerbate conflicts within the LGBTQ community. Scholars have documented that ways of expressing non-heteronormative identities vary depending on race and class, to name just two other categories. So for example, it may not be easy for a middle-class gay man in Mexico City to feel "solidarity" with a trans sex worker in a poor neighborhood (Domínguez-Ruvalcaba 2016). Ideas about feminism, womanhood, and lesbianism in Latin America may differ between a standard, middle-class "liberal," university-based version (Bellucci 2020) and an indigenous version (Duarte Bastian 2012, Picq 2018) or an Afro-Latin version (Curiel et al. 2005, González 2013, Dixon 2020). Intersectionalities matter because, as we will see, intra-movement divisions can play a role in whether the movement is successful or not in advancing its cause. An important challenge of the LGBTQ community in Latin America and the Caribbean is therefore upholding unity despite inherent divisions created by vast marginalized race, ethnic, and class subsections.

2 Conservative Dictatorships, Macho Marxists, and Uninterested Secularists: The 1960s and 1970s

The struggle for LGBTQ rights in Latin America and the Caribbean, as in the North Atlantic, became political in the 1960s. This decade, often thought of as the era of the sexual revolution – when the seeds for the gay liberation movement were planted worldwide (Weeks 2007) – posed a problem for Latin American LGBTQ activists that was less relevant in the North Atlantic: rising or returning authoritarianism. The region became plagued by military regimes that were staunchly repressive of homosexual activity and expression. Though homosexuality was legal in many countries, these regimes established decency codes of conduct that were used to target LGBTQ people. Targeting meant not just applying labor discrimination, but often arrest and torture. Private homosexuality might have been legal, but public indecency, and thus "homosexuality as a social practice," remained banned (Nesvig 2001:714). Although the designation LGBTQ was not common back then, and even the idea of gay pride was very new, homophobia was pervasive.

Green (2012, 2019) has argued that the rise of repression and censorship was inhumane, no doubt, but also generative, at least in Brazil. This authoritarian landscape was inhumane because LGBTQ people faced a predicament – they had to make greater efforts to stay in the closet to escape persecution. They could try to ingratiate themselves with the left, but given the authoritarian nature of the regime, this often meant joining insurrectionist movements, which was inherently dangerous or too involved. In other words, safety meant confronting unpleasant choices. However, the repression was generative in that gays and lesbians began to form communities and awareness of their stigmatized status. The rise of community under duress occurred initially within the confines of the closet (in secret gathering places), but eventually in more public settings, as the first modern homosexual movements begin to emerge in Latin America.

Thus, these early organizations emerged in response to both the international sexual revolution and repression coming from dictatorships (Facchini and França 2013). They were the first set of organizations that began to think of gay liberation as a democratic right and a human right. The problem, of course, was that groups were small and faced huge obstacles to meet and express themselves. Consciousness expanded even if movement reach remained circumscribed.

Part of the predicament of the politics of sexuality in Latin America in the 1960s was that the left, which was leading the fight against military juntas, was not entirely receptive to LGBTQ concerns either and, in fact, also projected homophobia (Simonetto 2017).[4] The strand of the left that was more inclined toward Marxism and the Cuban Revolution saw LGBTQ demands as a form of "bourgeois decadence" (Leiner 1994, Green 2012, McGee and Kampwirth 2015) and a sign of cultural imperialism, and thus worthy of repudiation. In Cuba, in particular, labor camps were established for gay men. When they were abolished, "dangerousness" laws remained in place which were systematically used to target LGBTQ citizens (Leiner 1994), including internment camps for HIV-infected people and counterrevolutionaries in the 1980s, making Castro's dictatorship one of the most homophobic places in Latin America (Arenas 1992,

---

[4] Leftist parties were arguably unreceptive even to some of the simple demands from feminists well into the late 1990s. See Friedman (2009).

Lumsden 1996). The strand of the left that was more influenced by Catholic social thought was less disdainful than the Marxist/Fidelista camp, but it still embraced the Church's teaching about the sinfulness of homosexual activity.

Regardless of the strand, the left prioritized macho performances in the 1960s and 1970s: rights were seen mostly in terms of economic gains that should go mostly to the (male) proletariat or those eager to pick up arms to fight for revolution. Women willing to adopt masculinized causes (either working for proletariat rights or embracing the armed struggle) were welcome. Men choosing alternative identities were seen as less useful, maybe even an inconvenience, a distraction, and in some cases as a frivolity that did not deserve rights. The Sandinista revolution in Nicaragua, after an initial period of incorporation of LGBTQ leaders, ended up crushing the movement in 1987 by order of the Ministry of the Interior (Thayer 1997, McGee and Kampwirth 2015). Some have faulted revolutionary regimes for groundless triumphalism when it comes to feminism, meaning that these regimes feel they have embraced all the pressing needs of women, that no other force treats these issues better, and that there is no need to keep insisting on further progress or even offer criticism (Mogrovejo 1996).

Others have argued, however, that some degree of tolerance, at least in some circles, contributed to early gay organizing in the 1960s. Ben and Insausti (2017), for instance, argue that in Argentina in the 1960s, while it was common for people to pathologize homosexuality, for the police to harass gays, and for upper-class gay men to live in fear, there was some degree of tolerance for blue-collar workers. Anti-capitalist unions were less hostile than one would think, permitting some form of gay socializing. This "socializing transitioned to political organization," once the military regime and the second Peronist administration became more intolerant. In addition, gay liberation movements gravitated toward alternative spaces that were far more welcoming: feminism, Trotskyism, and "contracultural" artistic circles (Simonetto 2017). In Mexico, gay movements also established closer ties with U.S. groups (Simonetto 2017).

The cultural and very machista distinction often made in Latin America, both within heterosexual and homosexual circles, between the active and the passive also provided some cover to some gay and bisexual men. Men seen as active and thus more masculine, or more able to sustain heterosexual relations, were less stigmatized than men who were passive and thus more feminine (Murray 1995a, 1995b, Prieur 1998). And in prerevolutionary Cuba, Havana itself offered some protections. The Catholic Church in Cuba was institutionally weaker, and thus less influential, than in the rest of Latin America (Crahan 1989), and santería, a leading Afro-Cuban religion, was welcoming of LGBTQ people and expressions (Morad 2008). Havana itself was a cosmopolitan city where "almost anything that was prohibited on the puritanical mainland of North America became possible" and thus LGBTQ expressions, especially in poor neighborhoods, were less stigmatized, with plenty of cruising areas and hook-up places for men (Lumsden 1996:33). However, despite or perhaps because of that tolerance, LGBTQ political organizing did not exist in Havana (or has not been researched yet).

In countries where more moderate regimes existed (Venezuela, Colombia, Costa Rica, and even Mexico), some early organizing of lesbian and gay groups took place. Lesbo-feminism became an organized movement in Mexico in the 1970s, for instance, and its key slogan was "*por un socialismo sin sexismo*" (Mogrovejo 2000), illustrating a commitment to anti-capitalism, anti-colonialism, and feminism. But the main challenge in these more moderate regimes was that secular leaders were often not that secular, meaning, they valued making concessions to religious actors and Christian Democratic parties or were simply unaccepting of the more modern notion of sexual citizenship, defined as the idea that the state needs to create the right socioeconomic, political, and health conditions for citizens to enjoy consensual sexual relations and voluntary gender expressions.[5]

Prior to the 1970s, the concept of sexual citizenship was absent from the discourse of human rights. Even the terms LGBTQ, and maybe even LGBTQ identities, let alone pride in them, were not widespread even among advocates. By the same token, pro-LGBTQ groups in democracies such as Costa Rica and Venezuela might not have felt in dire need to become too radical, given that the state traditionally guaranteed open spaces to civil society (Mogrovejo 1996, Thayer 1997, Ramos 2015). In the other cases, the state might have been too preoccupied with other threats. In semi-democratic Colombia, for instance, the state was at war with guerrillas. This took up much of the time and resources of the state. Consequently, little attention was paid to the spread of hate crimes (Bueno-Hansen 2017), what Serrano-Amaya (2018) has categorized as "sexual para-politics."

Overall, the most important advancement for LGBTQ rights during this period could very well have been the emergence of gay and lesbian identities *independent of* other forms of identity typical of the time (worker, feminist, Christian Democrat, activist, nationalist, Marxist, anarchist, middle-class, mixed-race, etc.). Without a "gay and lesbian" identity, a broad LGBTQ movement would not have emerged due to myriad ideological, class, and race differences separating the different groups that typically form part of any LGBTQ community (see Gamson 1995, Brown 2002).

---

[5] For a review of different conceptualizations of sexual citizenship, see Richardson 2017.

3 Democracy, Economic Crisis, and AIDS: Mid-1980s to Early 2000s

One would think that the transition to democracy in the region would be a godsend for LGBTQ movements. In many ways, it was. Suddenly, states and political parties became open defenders of human rights, pluralism, and freedom of expression. All of this created unheard-of opportunities for the LGBTQ community to organize and express itself. By 2000, most countries had already held their first Gay Pride (see Table 1). The LGBTQ community began to diversify its agenda and base, allying with other social movements, political parties, and international organizations, as well as making room for demands stemming not just from gay men, but from other members of the LGBTQ community. In particular, lesbians became more active and organized. They began to organize their own conference meetings (Encuentros Feministas Lésbicos Abya Yala).[6]

But in some ways, the rise of majoritarian-inclined institutions created new problems for movements that were minoritarian and stigmatized, to the point where some scholars have actually suggested that the vibrancy, if not the

Table 1 History of Gay Pride (date of first public march)

Country	Year
Mexico	1979
Colombia	1982
Nicaragua	1991
Argentina, Chile, Uruguay	1992
Brazil	1995
El Salvador, Venezuela	1997
Ecuador	1998
Dominican Republic	1999
Guatemala, Honduras, Bolivia	2000
Peru	2002
Costa Rica, Paraguay	2003
Panama	2005

Source: Adapted from Kollman and Sagarzazu (2017).

---

[6] Mexico, 1987; Costa Rica, 1990; Puerto Rico, 1992; Argentina, 1995; Brazil, 1999; Mexico, 2004; Chile, 2007; Guatemala, 2010; Bolivia, 2012; Colombia, 2014.

number, of pro-LGBTQ movements in the region might have declined or plateaued during the first decades of the transition to democracy.

The first problem was that the rise of democracy was a mixed blessing for LGBTQ concerns. On the one hand, state-directed homophobia lessened (though it did not disappear since in many places police forces harassed LGBTQ spaces). Censorship did decline, which allowed LGBTQ groups to communicate with other potential members and society at large. New public spaces became more amenable. On the other hand, democratization produced an avalanche of competing interest groups and parties clamoring for other policy priorities preferred by majorities. In Brazil, for instance, a pro-LGBTQ organization emerged (Triângulo Rosa) to influence the drafting of the new constitution in 1988, but did not achieve much other than the inclusion of the term *orientacão sexual* as one of the protected categories against discrimination. In addition, majoritarian rule – in a context in which homophobic attitudes prevailed – meant that it was very difficult for LGBTQ groups to have much bargaining leverage vis-à-vis large political parties. Democracy made some ruling parties even more susceptible to larger conservative constituencies or more powerful veto forces like the Catholic Church, and sometimes, they even regressed on LGBTQ issues. Carlos Menem in Argentina (Díez 2015, Encarnación 2015), for instance, and Violeta Chamorro in Nicaragua (McGee and Kampwirth 2015), adopted notoriously antigay positions and legislations, respectively.[7]

The second problem was that the concept of sexual citizenship remained unrecognized by most governments and political parties. While homosexuality was decriminalized, states continued to turn a blind eye to homophobia. Often, repressive practices continued. The Ecuador Truth Commission (2008–09), for instance, found that the Municipality of Guayaquil's "More Security" plan implemented in 2000 subjected LGBTQ individuals and groups to detentions, torture, and cruel treatment. Privately run and unregulated conversion therapy clinics proliferated in many Latin American countries; these clinics employed unethical, counterproductive, and abusive medical and psychological "treatments," often to nonconsenting minors (ILGA World: Ramon Mendos 2020).[8] In Colombia, hate crimes against LGBTQ forces continued to be perpetrated by both state forces and guerrillas even after the highly

---

[7] For instance, Menem boasted "that there are no militant gays and lesbians" in his party; his AIDS policy was weak and often relied on gay stereotypes; and he had frequent contact with the Vatican. Due to heavy lobbying pressure by activists, Menem eventually legalized CHA (Encarnación 2015).

[8] As of 2020, only Brazil and Ecuador have explicit laws banning conversion therapy. And in most countries, churches enjoy autonomy to engage in conversion therapy under the guise of religious education.

democratizing Constitution of 1991 (Bueno-Hansen 2017). In Argentina, arrests at gay clubs were made months after the democratic election of Raúl Alfonsín. His successor, Carlos Menem, displayed "overt hostility toward homosexuality," producing one of the most challenging times for the gay rights movement in the post-transition period (Encarnación 2015:118). In Bolivia in 1995, the police raided Cherry, a well-known gay bar, presumably searching for drugs.[9] The first gay pride march in 2000 was met by bands of homophobes throwing rocks at marchers.[10]

Furthermore, during much of this period, democratic governments were uninterested in antagonizing the Catholic Church. Aware as they were of all the other points of conflict with conservative actors, especially the military, new democracies did not want to open a battlefront with another conservative actor. This accommodation with the Church occurred at a time when the Vatican was actually turning more hardline on gay rights. In 1986, the Vatican issued a famous letter to bishops on "the problem of homosexuality," where, in response to calls within and outside the Church for more tolerance, the Vatican reiterated that homosexual behavior was to be rejected for going against "the creative wisdom of God" (Ratzinger 1986).[11]

In addition, this period came with two additional challenges for LGBTQ rights: the economic crisis and the AIDS crisis. The economic crisis covering the so-called "lost decade" of the 1980s, and for some countries, extending into the 2000s, meant that states faced social problems such as poverty, inflation, unreliable state services, crime explosion, and underinvestment that to vast majorities of the electorate were more urgent than LGBTQ themes. Some initial breakthroughs in the politics of LGBTQ rights had to be interrupted in the 1980s due to the economic crisis (e.g., McGee and Kampwirth 2015). In Venezuela, for instance, LGBTQ activism declined in the 1980s: the pro-gay movement Entendidos, established in 1975, discontinued publishing its magazine in 1983 (Ramos 2015). In Cuba, the first reassignment surgery was conducted in 1988, but the program was suspended for the next twenty years in response to the economic crisis that followed the collapse of the Soviet Union (Kirk and Huish 2018).

---

[9] www.refworld.org/docid/3ae6abdd0.html.

[10] www.facebook.com/RevistaEgoBolivia/posts/1736470316634231.

[11] A second document from the Vatican in 2003 entitled "Considerations Regarding Proposals to Give Legal Recognition to Unions Between Homosexual Persons" reiterated this position: "The Church teaches that respect for homosexual persons cannot lead in any way to approval of homosexual behaviour or to legal recognition of homosexual unions." www.vatican.va/roman_curia/congregations/cfaith/documents/rc_con_cfaith_doc_20030731_homosexual-unions_en.html. The document was authored by Cardinal Ratzinger (future Pope Benedict) and approved by then-Pope John Paul II.

Then there was the AIDS crisis. As Youde (2020:302) states, the world as a whole responded initially to the AIDS crisis with "apathy and antipathy." Latin America was no exception. Many groups used the pretext of AIDS to express and intensify their homophobia. The Catholic Church, along with many politicians, often made the argument that AIDS was a divine punishment. Even when they avoided stigmatizing discourse and supported important charity work for AIDS patients, the clergy often embraced policies that made containment strategies difficult to achieve, such as rejecting the use of condoms, sex education, and needle-sharing programs (Smallman 2007). Furthermore, governments were often too eager to let the Catholic Church deal the health-care crisis prompted by the HIV/AIDS epidemic so that they didn't have to provide relief themselves. This off-loading made governments and civil society unwilling to criticize the Church's ambivalence on the subject: while preaching and practicing "mercy and charity" toward the HIV/AIDS community, the Church was still proposing homophobic or unhelpful positions (for Brazil, see Murray et al. 2011).

The one positive aspect of the AIDS epidemic was that international aid organizations encouraged or even forced governments in unlikely places to interact with the gay community and create outreach programs. Ministries of health, for instance, were often compelled to promote gay health centers. In 1988, USAID awarded the Bolivian Ministry of Health a three-year $500,000 assistance grant to begin HIV/AIDS surveillance and education effort that led to a gay men's outreach center in Santa Cruz (Wright 2000).

To their credit, LGBTQ groups in Latin America managed to find or deploy successful tools to handle these challenges. One such tool was to seek alliances with larger social movements, even political parties (Facchini 2003, de la Dehesa 2010). By seeking greater ties with parties and movements of the left, the LGBTQ community helped make many leftist movements more sympathetic to LGBTQ causes. The second was alliances with bureaucrats. The AIDS crisis compelled LGBTQ movements to lobby and build alliances with ministries of health and international organizations (Altman 1999, Frasca 2005, de la Dehesa 2010, Torres-Ruiz 2011, McGee and Kampwirth 2015). This type of close project-based collaboration between ministries of health and social movements occurred in both rich/large countries such as Brazil (Gomez 2010, Friedman and Tabbush 2019, Matos 2019) as well as poorer/smaller countries such as El Salvador and Ecuador (International Human Rights Law Clinic 2012, Cardona Acuña 2019). In all instances, this collaboration led not just to stronger health responses, but also stronger protections from discrimination in health sectors.

Political parties during this period were not totally receptive to LGBTQ movements. However, international organizations ended up working closely with, and even borrowing strategies from, local LGBTQ groups on how to frame issues to raise awareness and, ultimately, acceptance. LGBTQ rights movements generated the framework that gay rights = human rights/civil rights (Encarnación 2018). In partnership with international organizations, they were able to bolster this argument by advancing the frame: gay rights = health rights = citizen rights (Smallman 2007). Likewise, international organizations facilitated the creation of open spaces for LGBTQ movements to operate domestically (Youde 2020).

Another important development during this period involved huge strides by international feminism. Rising feminism in the 1980s encouraged lesbians not only to get organized but also to seek some distance from the radical left of the 1960s and embrace instead a discourse in favor of "diversity" and "distinctiveness" that was uncommon in the 1960s and 1970s when a more typical theme was "*liberación homosexual*" (Mogrovejo 2000).

At the same time, this period also reveals limitations or complications associated with some of the institutional approaches of the time. Alliances with feminists to influence processes of constitutional rewrite (in Brazil, Argentina, Colombia, and Venezuela) might have succeeded in changing the text and thus the nation from a "heterosexual contract" into a new "estado-nación-multicultural y pluricultural," but stopped short of granting ample LGBTQ rights (Curiel 2013). Collaborations with specific ministries did expand protections and tolerance, but often in limited circumscriptions (e.g., health sectors) and at the risk of too much co-optation, which could end up "taming once-radical" groups (McGee and Kampwirth 2015). These collaborations were often insufficient to produce enduring legislation.

In addition, LGBTQ movements in Brazil and Mexico tried to establish ties with parties only to discover risks (see Brown 2002, Marsiaj 2006, de la Dehesa 2010, Encarnación 2015): if allied parties were too small, LGBTQ groups could obtain large influence within that party but not so much across the country. If allied parties were large (e.g., PT in Brazil), LGBTQ groups faced the challenge of having to compete for influence with larger constituencies within the party, including religious groups (Marsiaj 2006). In Nicaragua and Mexico, for instance, ties between LGBTQ movements and large parties (Sandinistas and the PRI) provided "visibility without rights" (McGee and Kampwirth 2015). And if the system was too polarized, ties with a party could give LGBTQ groups unnecessary enemies from parties on the other side. Consequently, some LGBTQ groups opted not to focus on ties with parties. Likewise, LGBTQ groups experienced the pitfalls of international collaboration.[12] The most important type of international

---

[12] A related theme is transnational diffusion of ideas and how LGBTQ movements took and adapted cues from cases abroad. See Friedman (2012).

collaboration of the time focused on AIDS, which meant that perhaps too much emphasis was being placed on the "men-who-have-sex-with-men" community to the chagrin of other concerns and constituencies of the LGBTQ community.

In short, this was a period of enormous innovations in interactions between LGBTQ movements and other movements, ministries, political parties, and international organizations, but the results in terms of expanding rights or even changing homophobic public opinion were for the most part modest.

4 The Rights Explosion of the 2000s

In the 2003–13 period, things cleared up a bit for LGBTQ politics. Latin America was able to solve many of the macroeconomic problems of the past. The AIDS crisis stopped being an all-consuming issue for the gay community. Poverty declined. Groups calling for new forms of participatory democracy gained power. Politicians began to understand better the notion of sexual citizenship. In addition, LGBTQ organizing experienced a boom in several countries. In Mexico, for instance, pro-LGBTQ groups expanded from approximately ten nationwide in 1990 to nearly forty in Mexico City alone by 2000 (Díez 2015). All these changes created conditions for what could very well be described as the most important transformation of the legal environment for LGBTQ people in the history of the world outside of the North Atlantic.

The LGBTQ politics during this period focused on these main topics: (1) stronger and broader antidiscrimination policies and ordinances, including hate crime laws; (2) more proactive policies to educate elected officials, civil servants, school teachers and staff, health providers, the police, and the population at large; (3) changes to civil codes to ensure rights for same-sex families (*matrimonio igualitario, familias homoparentales y diversas, derechos patrimoniales*);[13] and (4) gender identity recognition for trans and intersex people.

Table 2 shows the expansion of three of the most important and controversial changes in Latin America: civil unions, marriage rights, and trans-inclusive gender identity laws starting in 2006. In 2020, eight countries offered civil unions for same-sex couples; six countries and many parts of Mexico offered same-sex marriage, and nine offered gender identity laws.

Table 3 covers some of the most important LGBTQ rights granted by country as of 2020. Three features are worth noting. First, rights include more than just marriage rights. Second, the transformation has been uneven. In some countries, progress has been significant (Argentina, Chile, Brazil, Mexico, Chile, Costa Rica, Colombia); in others, progress has been partial (Cuba, Bolivia, El

---

[13] In Portuguese: *casamento igualitario, famílias homoparentais (homoparentalidade), direitos patrimoniais.*

Table 2 Expansion of same-sex civil unions, marriage, and gender identity laws, 2006–2020

The Rise of Civil Unions, Civil Marriage, and Gender Identity Laws

	2006	2007	2008	2009	2010	2011	2012	2013	2014	2015	2016	2017	2018	2019	2020
													Chile	Chile	Chile
													Brazil	Brazil	Brazil
												Mexico	Mexico	Mexico	Mexico
												Peru	Peru	Peru	Peru
											Ecuador	Ecuador	Ecuador	Ecuador	Ecuador
											Bolivia	Bolivia	Bolivia	Bolivia	Bolivia
							Argentina	Argentina	Argentina	Argentina	Argentina	Argentina	Argentina	Argentina	Argentina
				Uruguay	Uruguay	Uruguay	Uruguay	Uruguay	Uruguay	Uruguay	Uruguay	Uruguay	Uruguay	Uruguay	Uruguay
Panama	Panama	Panama	Panama	Panama	Panama	Panama	Panama	Panama	Panama	Panama	Panama	Panama	Panama	Panama
															Costa Rica
															Ecuador
										Colombia	Colombia	Colombia	Colombia	Colombia
							Uruguay	Uruguay	Uruguay	Uruguay	Uruguay	Uruguay	Uruguay	Uruguay	Uruguay
							Brazil	Brazil	Brazil	Brazil	Brazil	Brazil	Brazil	Brazil	Brazil
					Mexico*	Mexico*	Mexico*	Mexico*	Mexico*	Mexico*	Mexico*	Mexico*	Mexico*	Mexico*	Mexico*
					Argentina	Argentina	Argentina	Argentina	Argentina	Argentina	Argentina	Argentina	Argentina	Argentina	Argentina
									Chile	Chile	Chile	Chile	Chile	Chile	Chile
								Costa Rica	Costa Rica	Costa Rica	Costa Rica	Costa Rica	Costa Rica	Costa Rica
					Brazil	Brazil	Brazil	Brazil	Brazil	Brazil	Brazil	Brazil	Brazil	Brazil	Brazil
				Mexico	Mexico	Mexico	Mexico	Mexico	Mexico	Mexico	Mexico	Mexico	Mexico	Mexico
			Ecuador	Ecuador	Ecuador	Ecuador	Ecuador	Ecuador	Ecuador	Ecuador	Ecuador	Ecuador	Ecuador	Ecuador
		Argentina	Argentina	Argentina	Argentina	Argentina	Argentina	Argentina	Argentina	Argentina	Argentina	Argentina	Argentina	Argentina
	Uruguay	Uruguay	Uruguay	Uruguay	Uruguay	Uruguay	Uruguay	Uruguay	Uruguay	Uruguay	Uruguay	Uruguay	Uruguay	Uruguay
	Colombia	Colombia	Colombia	Colombia	Colombia	Colombia	Colombia	Colombia	Colombia	Colombia	Colombia	Colombia	Colombia	Colombia

Legend:
- Gender Identity Laws
- Same Sex Marriage Legalized
- Same-Sex Civil Unions Recognized

* Mexico legalized same-sex marriage first in the Federal District; by 2020, it is available in 18 of 31 states. It's gender identity law refers to reduce restrictions for voting

Source: Corrales's LGBT Timeline of LGBT Rights in the Americas.

Table 3 The expansion of LGBTQ rights in Latin America and the Caribbean

Country	Homosexual activity (a)	Anti discrimination law (b)	Military service (c)	Gender identity protection (d)	Name/gender change in nat'l docs (e)	Hate crime legislation (f)	Recognition of same-sex relationships (g)	Same-sex marriage (h)	Adoption for same-sex couples (i)
Argentina	Yes (1887)	Yes (1988)	Yes (2009)	Yes (2012)	Yes (2012)	Yes (2012)	Yes (2008)	Yes (2010)	Yes (2010)
Brazil	Yes (1830)	Yes (2019)	Yes******	Yes (2019)	Yes (2018)	Yes (2019)	Yes (2011)	Yes (2013)	Yes (2010)
Colombia	Yes (1981)	Yes (2011)	Yes (1999)	Yes (2015)	Yes (2015)	Yes (2000)	Yes (2007)	Yes (2016)	Yes (2015)
Uruguay	Yes (1934)	Yes (2003)	Yes (2009)	Yes (2003)	Yes (2009)	Yes (2003)	Yes (2007)	Yes (2013)	Yes (2009)
Costa Rica	Yes (1971)	Yes (1998)	N/A*	Yes (1998)	Yes (2018)	No	Yes (2014)	Yes (2020)	Yes (2020)
Chile	Yes (1999)	Yes (2012)	Yes (2012)	Yes (2012)	Yes (2018)	Yes (2012)	Yes (2015)	No****	No*****
Ecuador	Yes (1997)	Yes (1998)	No	Yes (1998)	Yes (2016)	Yes (2009)	Yes (2009)	Yes (2019)	No
Mexico	Yes (1872)	Yes (2003)	Yes******	Yes (2003)	**	Yes (2014)	Yes (2010)	**	**
Bolivia	Yes (1832)	Yes (2009)	Yes (2013)	Yes (2009)	Yes (2016)	Yes (2010)	No	No	No

Table 3 (cont.)

Country	Homosexual activity (a)	Anti discrimination law (b)	Military service (c)	Gender identity protection (d)	Name/gender change in nat'l docs (e)	Hate crime legislation (f)	Recognition of same-sex relationships (g)	Same-sex marriage (h)	Adoption for same-sex couples (i)
El Salvador	Yes (1822)	Yes (2018)	Yes******	Yes (2018)	No	Yes (2015)	No	No	No
Guatemala	Yes (1871)	No	Yes******	No	Yes***** (2016)	No	No	No	No
Peru	Yes (1924)	Yes (2017)	Yes*** (2009)	Yes (2017)	Yes (2016)	No	No	No	No
Cuba	Yes (1979)	Yes (2019)	Yes (1993)	Yes (2019)	Yes (2013)	No	No	No	No
Nicaragua	Yes (2008)	Yes (2014)	No	Yes (2014)	No	Yes (2008)	No	No	No
Honduras	Yes (1899)	Yes (2013)	Yes******	No	No	No	No	No	No
Venezuela	Yes (1997)	Yes (2012)	No	Partial**	No	No	No	No	No
Panama	Yes (2008)	No	N/A*	No	No	No	No	No	No
Paraguay	Yes (1880)	No	Yes******	No	No	No	No	No	No
Dom. Rep.	Yes (1822)	No	No	No	No	No	No	No	No

Spanish not main language.

Country									
Belize	Yes (2016)	Yes (2016)	No	Yes (2016)	No	No	No	No	No
Bahamas	Yes (1991)	No	Yes (1998)	No	No	No	No	No	No
Suriname	Yes (1811)	Yes (2015)	No	No	No	No	No	No	No
Jamaica	No	No	No	No	No	No	No	No	No
Guyana	No	No	Yes (2012)	No	No	No	No	No	No
Haiti	Yes (1791)	No	N/A*	No	No	No	No	No	No
Trinidad and Tobago	Yes (2018)	No	No	No	No	No	No	No	No
Barbados	No	No	No	No	No	No	No	No	No
United States	Yes (2003)	Partial**	Yes*** (2011)	Partial**	Partial**	Partial**	Yes (2015)	Yes (2015)	Yes (2016)

Notes:

*   No standing military

**   Legal on a state by state basis

***   No for trans people

**** Legislation to legalizing being debated and appears likely to pass

***** Name change but not gender

****** No known law prohibiting LGBTQ persons from serving in military

(a) Same-sex sexual activity fully depenalized for both genders.

(b) Strong legal protections against discrimination based on sexual orientation.

(c) Homosexuals allowed to serve in the military.

(d) Strong legal protections against discrimination for gender identity.

(e) Change national legal documents to confirm gender identity and name without precondition of surgery.

(f) Laws exist to prosecute crimes targeting people for being LGBTQ or appearing to be LGBTQ.

(g) Same-sex relationships legally recognized.

(h) Equal rights of marriage extended to same-sex couple as heterosexual couples.

(i) Homosexuals enjoy same rights to adopt children as heterosexuals.

Sources: Corrales (2020a), ILGA World: Ramon Mendos (2019), Malta e al. (2019), table 1.

Salvador, Guatemala, Peru, Nicaragua) or even minimal (Panama, Paraguay, the Dominican Republic, and most non-Spanish-speaking Caribbean nations).

An important development within the LGBTQ movement in this period involved greater recognition of intersectionalities. This was especially true within the lesbo-feminist movement. In the 1990s, for instance, in conjunction with debates about the 500th anniversary of Columbus's landing, lesbian groups began to bring attention to certain *"ausencias,"* referring to forms of representation that had been missing from liberal and socialist forms of feminisms, specifically, afro, indigenous, "popular," and even trans lesbo-feminisms. The official replacement in the early 2010s of the name "Latinoamericano y Caribeño" to "Abya Yala" in an important regional lesbian-feminist organization is representative of this growing awareness of intersectionalities (Encuentro Lésbico Feminista de Abya Yala 2016).[14]

Also in the 1990s, especially in Brazil, trans movements began to organize autonomously. In 1992, the first political trans movement in Latin America and second in the world was established in Rio, Associação das Travestis e Liberados (ASTRAL) (Carvalho and Carrara 2013). Their primary concern was to combat police violence and arbitrary arrests of the trans community. From then on, the trans movement experienced a flourishing across the region.

5 The Rise of the Trans Movement

An important consequence of achieving advances in the legal provisions and awareness of intersectionality among LGBTQ movements has been an expansion of opportunities to focus on newer demands. One such demand concerns trans rights.

Trans lives and communities (as well as transphobia) have a long tradition in Latin America. Anthropologists, historians, and literary scholars have documented that Latin American societies have offered multiple examples of nonheteronormative sexual and gender expressions since pre-Columbian times, including third genders (Ben 2004) and sodomy (Nesvig 2001). But it was not until the 2000s that trans communities became better organized to place autonomous demands on the public agenda. And their legal victories typically came after sexual-orientation rights were obtained (Longaker and Haider-Markel 2014).

It is important to pause to discuss a bit the controversy, no longer salient, of the use of the term *trans*. Until the 1990s, most trans-identified people did not use the term trans. They preferred other terms such as transvestis/travesti, and

---

[14] Abya Yala is precolonial term used by an indigenous tribe from present-day Colombia and Panama to talk about their native lands (the continent).

many did not even consider this to be their most important identity (Carvalho and Carrara 2013). But in the late 1990s, in part as a response to the dominance of gay males as well as international pressure to adopt the term transgender, mostly from European international social movements, Brazilian trans people started to use the term trans while rejecting the term transgender.[15]

In Latin America, trans groups have focused on four main political goals, not necessarily in this order of preference. First, they want to raise awareness of their plight. The trans community faces high exposure to stigma, violence, labor discrimination, and illness. Many trans people report exclusion from their families and communities (Buriticá López 2013). They face enormous barriers to accessing formal employment or positions commensurate with their academic preparedness. Because of these barriers, they are overrepresented in informal labor markets. A study in Mexico showed that two of ten trans adults work in informal markets (Mejores Empleos 2019). Precarious living conditions explain why transgender women have a life expectancy of thirty-five years in Central America (RedLacTrans 2018), compared with seventy-five years for cisgender people in the region. Rates of HIV are forty-nine times higher for trans women than the general population, contributing to low life expectancy (see Figure 1). HIV status is a double-edged sword, incentivizing and blocking migration: recipient countries often use HIV status to deny visas (Mogrovejo 2018). Trans people in Latin America often face stigma from health-care systems, and consequently, underconsume health services (Malta et al. 2019).

Second, the movement seeks a cultural change: create awareness that gender identity is not biologically determined. Essentially, this means changing the idea that trans identity is a form of pathology or confusion ("¡*Despatologización de las Identidades Trans Ya!*"). While there has been some progress at the international level (in 2018, the World Health Organization stopped classifying trans identity as a mental illness) and in some countries (with Argentina and Uruguay as the countries with the most pro-trans legislation in the Americas), cultural attitudes remain transphobic. The organization RedLacTrans reports that approximately 77 percent of trans people are expelled from their homes and 25 percent stop their education based on harassment.

Third, the trans community has focused on obtaining the right to change gender identity in legal documents (e.g., birth certificates, passports, national ID cards, driver's licenses, voting ID cards, contracts, etc.) without the need for medical approval or transformation (Longaker and Haider-Markel 2014,

---

[15] In Brazil, the term transgender was rejected for at least two reasons. Many trans activists thought it gave too much leeway to people who transitioned back and forth between genders. Also, the term became too similar to the term "alimentos transgênicos," which became a popular stigmatizing term at the same time.

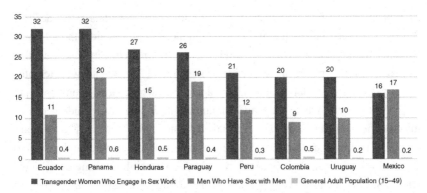

Figure 1 HIV prevalence in Latin America, by population segment, selected countries, 2013

Note: Data for men who have sex with men is the average in 2009–13.

Source: UNAIDS (2014).

Arrubia 2019, Adrián 2020). Not having the right identity in legal documents can block access to a number of public and private services and lead to awkward situations in public. Argentina's Gender Identity Law (2012), the first in the world to protect gender identity status and to call for free medical services for the trans community, has become a world standard. By early 2020, more than 9,000 people had changed their national ID document (Télam 2020).

And fourth, the movement is deeply committed to enhancing security for the trans community, in part because it is a community disproportionately targeted by both domestic and public hate crime. Trans people face murders at high rates, with 80 percent of global trans murders occurring in Latin America (Trans Murder Monitor 2019). Central and South America have recorded 2,608 cases of hate-related murders of trans people between 2008 and 2019, representing 78.6 percent of cases worldwide (Trans Murder Monitor 2019). Many times, trans murder victims also show signs of torture or physical abuse. Insecurity is often the result of transphobic hate crime, lack of police protection, and the fact that many trans people engage in sex work in the streets, where crime is high to begin with (RedLacTrans 2018). Police are often not reliable providers of security. Often, the police are both (underground) users of trans sex-work services, as well as the main victimizers of sex workers. Police violence has prompted trans activists to form organizations (International Human Rights Law Clinic 2012, RedLacTrans 2018). For this reason, a large number of trans crime victims choose not to report incidents to the police (Amnesty International 2017). For the trans community, security also involves health security and access to health services in general, not just access to gender-affirming medical practices (Winter et al. 2016). Around

52 percent report bad treatment in health clinics and hospitals (RedLacTrans 2018). Trans activists often point out the high incidence of suicidal thoughts and attempts among trans people: a 2011 survey in Mexico City revealed that 41 percent of trans people have considered suicide and 22 percent have attempted it (Garza 2018). In El Salvador and Nicaragua, trans women tend to end up in jail disproportionately, where they suffer innumerable indignities including gender misclassification, public mockery, sexual abuse, and being treated as "everyone's property" (Johnson et al. 2020). Studies suggest that trans people (and gay men) in the Northern Triangle countries have a higher probability of migrating to the United States than the average population, and during their journey, they are more likely to be targeted by criminal gangs and authorities; they are also more likely to be sexually assaulted during their journeys and in detention centers (Amnesty International 2017).

6 Explaining the Rise of LGBTQ Rights

The literature on LGBTQ rights has focused on not just documenting the history of LGBTQ rights movements, but also explaining it. Two questions in particular have been central. First, what was different about the post-2003 period relative to the previous ones? In the 1980s–90s, for instance, there was democracy and LGBTQ movements had ties with other social movements, parties, and international organizations, yet rights expanded slowly or not at all, whereas, in the most recent period, rights expanded rapidly. And second, why has the current expansion been so uneven, with some rights expanding in some areas and not others, and in some cases and not others? The following section reviews the strengths and weaknesses of various arguments offered.

6.1 Relaxations in the Religious Barrier

An important argument to explain the expansion of LGBTQ rights has to do with a change in religious attitudes. Two changes in religious conditions may have facilitated the expansion of LGBTQ rights in this period: the rise of irreligiosity and the rise of light Catholicism.

Irreligiosity refers to people who do not describe themselves as religious or identify with any particular religion (including atheists or agnostics) (Somma et al. 2017). In some countries, they represented more than 10 percent of the population in 2013 (Argentina, Chile, the Dominican Republic, Brazil, El Salvador, Nicaragua, Uruguay) (Latinobarómetro 2014, Somma et al. 2017). They tend to be liberal on issues of sexuality.

Light Catholicism refers to the rise of people who still identify as Catholic but are more relaxed about official church doctrine, especially concerning sexuality.

Light religiosity is significantly more prevalent among Catholics than Evangelicals (Corrales and Sagarzazu 2019). When asked about their views on homosexuality, a greater proportion of Catholics show far more acceptance than do Evangelicals (Chaux et al. 2021). In Uruguay, Argentina, Chile, Mexico, and Brazil, only a minority of Catholics disapprove same-sex marriage, suggesting a high incidence of light Catholicism (Figure 2). In a study of seven Latin American countries, Catholics were found to be "more tolerant of homosexuality than other religious groups" (Navarro et al. 2019:262).[16] Gonzalez-Rostani et al. (2020) document similar findings among legislators.

It could very well be that what's driving this rise of light religiosity among Catholics is the decline of "church attendance" (Smith and Boas 2020),

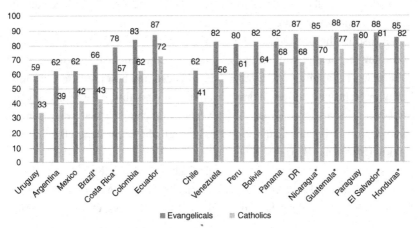

Figure 2 Percentage opposed to same-sex marriage by religion, 2014

Notes:

Countries where same-sex marriage are recognized: Uruguay, Argentina, Chile, Mexico, Brazil, Costa Rica, Colombia, and Ecuador.

* Country with large Protestant population (25 percent or higher identify as Protestant).

Source: Pew Research Center (2014).

---

[16] There has been speculation on whether Pope Francis is a light Catholic, or at least, a more compassionate Catholic regarding homosexuality. The evidence is contradictory. Shortly after the start of his papacy, Pope Francis stunned the world in 2013 by stating during an interview about gay priests that "If someone is gay and he searches for the Lord and has good will, who am I to judge?" He spoke in Italian but used the word "gay." However, he adopted intolerant attitudes subsequently, when he fired a Polish priest for coming out in 2015. Then in October 2020, Pope Francis made headlines again with the release of a new documentary on his life entitled "Francesco," in which he is quoted stating that homosexuals "have a right to a family" and that "what we have to create is a civil union law." While Pope Francis, before becoming Pope, was known in Argentina for supporting civil unions (and criticized for stopping short of endorsing same-sex marriage), this statement more recent suggests a departure from the predominant sentiment among the top clergy of the Church and even Church teaching, which calls on homosexuals to practice chastity and to refrain from adopting children.

disastisfaction with Church scandals related to clergy misconduct, or a decline in the degree of "importance attributed to religion" by specific individuals (Navarro et al. 2019). Again, this trend is dominant among Catholics and less so among Evangelicals. In a 2014 survey (Pew Research Center 2014), only 41 percent of Catholics in Latin America stated attending religious services "weekly," far lower than the average for Evangelicals at 72 percent.[17] Of course, here we face a typical chicken or egg question. Is decline in church attendance driving the rise of light Catholicism or is light Catholicism driving the decline in church attendance. Regardless of the answer, research shows that people who attend church services less tend to have more tolerant views about LGBTQ issues (Dion and Díez 2017), and Catholics attend church services less than do Evangelicals. It is no coincidence that countries with lower church attendance have been able to establish same-sex marriage (Dion and Díez 2017, Jackman 2017).

Because of the prevalence of light religiosity among Catholics now, it is becoming increasingly difficult to say that the Latin American electorate is still split between Catholics and Evangelicals. Instead, the best predictor of voting behavior, especially in questions pertaining to sexuality, is whether a voter "self-identifies as nonreligious and never attends church": that voter is more likely to vote left than a Catholic or Evangelical who attends church more than weekly (Smith and Boas 2020).

The prevalence of irreligiosity and light Catholicism can also help explain the difference between Latin America and the non-Spanish-speaking Caribbean. For the most part, the latter has lagged in offering LGBTQ rights. One reason for this lag is that most of these countries are intensely religious (Wilets 2010) – predominantly Evangelical with tiny Catholic populations (with the exception of Belize and Haiti). In addition, Evangelicalism in the Anglo-Caribbean is deeply connected to nationalism: during colonial times, it was Evangelical churches (rather than the Anglican church) that formed ties with slaves, siding with them during the emancipation struggle (in the nineteenth century) and with black anti-imperialists during the independence struggle (in the 1960s–80s) (Neel 2016). The Anglo-Caribbean, therefore, did not develop the type of anticlericalism that has always existed in Latin America. This may explain why citizens in these countries think of criticisms from abroad about their LGBTQ gaps as another example of "blacklighting" and react defensively with nationalist, anti-imperialist, and racial pride arguments (Grey and Attai 2020).

That said, it is important to notice the progress that even the Caribbean and Central America have made in the last decade. All of Central America has legalized homosexuality. Antidiscrimination ordinances are getting stronger.

---

[17] This gap declines significantly in El Salvador, Nicaragua, Honduras, and Guatemala.

And in the Anglo-Caribbean, Belize declared buggery laws unconstitutional, and Jamaica has developed an effective pro-LGBTQ social movement, J-FLAG, that has succeeded in getting politicians to focus on discrimination and pay more attention to homophobia (Faber 2018).

6.2 Limitations of the Religious Relaxation Hypothesis

It is important not to exaggerate the extent of religious opening in Latin America. Figure 2, for instance, reveals important outliers to the religious opening hypothesis: Colombia, Ecuador, Costa Rica, and Chile. In the former three cases, light Catholics are not majorities, and yet these countries achieved same-sex marriage. In Chile, in contrast, light Catholics are majorities, but the country has yet to achieve same-sex marriage (although the country did achieve recognition of civil unions and an equal-marriage bill is sitting in congress).

The reason why religion continues to act as a barrier even where the Catholic laity might be turning more tolerant is the existence of other trends in religion toward greater conservatism.

First, Evangelicals are expanding quickly in most countries, and in some (Brazil, Costa Rica, Nicaragua, Guatemala, El Salvador, and Honduras) they already account for more than 25 percent of the population.[18] The problem for LGBTQ rights is that Evangelicals, both clergy and laity, tend to be intensely conservative on LGBTQ issues, more so than Catholics (Chaux et al. 2021, Corrales and Sagarzazu 2019). Doctrinally, at least, the Catholic Church has at times been "more accepting" of LGBTQ people than other Christian faiths, creating, for instance, same-sex communities (monasteries and nunneries) and making a distinction between homosexual desire (acceptable) and homosexual acts (unacceptable) (Summers 2004). Evangelicals are not only more dogmatic on LGBTQ issues, but also more organized and have deep roots across society (Malamud 2018, Zilla 2018, Corrales and Sagarzazu 2019, Smith 2019, Boas 2021). Corrales (2020) examines Evangelical churches using analytical tools designed to evaluate the relative political strength of NGOs, and concludes that in terms of unity, ability to raise funds, reach across classes and sectors, ability to expand, and connectedness to constituents (church goers), there is no other NGO (and possibly institution) in Latin America that can rival Evangelicals. While Evangelicals have strong ties to low-income

---

[18] In Latin America, most people who identify as Protestant belong to either an Evangelical or a Pentecostal church, rather than a mainline Protestant church. In comparison to mainline Protestants, Evangelicals/Pentecostals tend to interpret the Bible more literally, place greater emphasis on the "born again" experience in which the individual needs to make a strong commitment to follow religious teachings, emphasize in their theology the idea that Jesus Christ is a spiritual and physical healer, and often prefer charismatic preachers in their worship (see Garrard 2019).

communities, they also keep especially close ties to wealthy sectors of society. Evangelicals famously embrace the so-called prosperity theory, which states that personal wealth is God's reward for living a Christian life, so they feel comfortable endorsing positions by the wealthy class (Garrard 2019). Evangelical influence is also supported by a powerful transnational network. One important example is the World Congress of Families (WCF), a US-based organization with links to the U.S. Christian Right that serves as an umbrella organization for a massive network of organizations pushing against LGBTQ rights (see www.splcenter.org/fighting-hate/extremist-files/group/world-congress-families). Velasco (2020) has found that the frequency, geographic scope, and levels of attendance of meetings of the WCF are expanding rapidly, and thus, its ability to rival and even contain liberal transnational forces advocating for LGBTQ rights (see also Velasco 2019).

Second, the Catholic clergy, which is still an important mobilizer of public opinion, has become even more conservative. The clergy has turned less progressive on social issues and more conservative on sexuality issues (Daudelin and Hewitt 1995, Hagopian 2008, Htun 2009, Marcus-Delgado 2020), even if it has become more relaxed on other "sins" such as divorce, premarital sex, and adultery. In many ways, the very intolerant attitudes of contemporary Evangelicalism toward sexuality are being (re)adopted by the Catholic clergy.

Finally, the main problem with using declining religiosity as an independent variable to explain pro-LGBTQ changes is that we are not entirely sure of the direction of causality. One could posit that expansion of irreligiosity and light Catholicism might be more an effect than a cause of the success of pro-LGBTQ forces in generating cultural change and widespread tolerance.

Because religion remains a strong barrier, it is important to go beyond religion. Most of the scholarship on this camp draws heavily from social-movement theory and institutionalism. In what follows, I offer examples of some of the most important arguments that have been advanced to explain success in a given case or cases.

6.3 Parties and Presidents

An important topic of research has been how exactly do (ruling) parties help the LGBTQ cause, if at all. During the transition to democracy of the 1980s, LGBTQ movements in Latin America encountered problems when trying to work with parties on the left (see Section 3). But some scholars wondered if those party-related problems stemmed from the fact that back then leftist parties were in the opposition, and whether the relationship with those parties would improve if they became governing parties. There is some evidence that leftist parties in power were more receptive to some progressive and even feminist concerns, especially with respect to women's representation (Friedman 2009), than they were in the past and in relation to other parties. In Argentina, Uruguay, and Costa Rica, same sex-marriage was certainly advanced by ruling parties on the left. However, it seems that the ruling party's ideological orientation matters less than the degree of interparty competition and the regime's commitment to transparency, accountability, and the rule of law, and the latter two factors seem to matter more in high-income or urbanized countries (Friedman and Tabbush 2019).

The evidence on behalf of the importance of leftist ruling party ideology as a predictor of LGBTQ rights is not strong. On the one hand, it is true that right-wing ruling parties strongly aligned with conservative religious groups (e.g., Alberto Fujimori in Peru, Álvaro Uribe in Colombia, Jair Bolsonaro in Brazil, Jimmy Morales in Guatemala, Horacio Cartes in Paraguay) never come out in favor of expanding LGBTQ rights (see Marsiaj 2006). On the other hand, many left-leaning ruling parties have faltered, at least on the question of family rights (Schulenberg 2013, Gonzalez-Rostani et al. 2020). González-Rostani et al. (2020) find that except in Uruguay, parties on the left and center-left had many legislators who were not necessarily supportive of same-sex marriage; religiosity, more than ideology, explains legislators' position on same-sex marriage. This may explain why, during Latin America's so-called left turn (1999–2010s), ruling-party support for same-sex marriage was not automatic.

For instance, the new constitutions in Venezuela (1999), Ecuador (2008), and Bolivia (2009) touted by the left as highly participatory and sensitive to leftist ideologies, include blatant heteronormative articles (Articles 77, 67, and 63, respectively) that define marriage explicitly in binary terms. There is reason to believe that these articles were introduced with the explicit intention of blocking marriage equality (Merentes 2010, Xie and Corrales 2010, Garriga-López 2016, Adrián 2020). Many leftist ruling parties needed to be pressured hard by social movements and international actors to move forward with LGBTQ rights. And still, many of them failed to support same-sex marriage through legislation (e.g., Lula da Silva in Brazil, Laura Chinchilla in Costa Rica). Others offered weak support (Michelle Bachelet in Chile sent a same-sex marriage bill only seven months before the end of her second term). Others blocked or ignored the issue (Hugo Chávez in Venezuela, Ollanta Humala and Alan García in Peru, Danilo Medina in the Dominican Republic, Salvador Sánchez Cerén in El Salvador). And still others actually backtracked, turning more conservative, less pro-LGBTQ, or more conditional with time (Rafael Correa in Ecuador, Evo Morales in Bolivia, Daniel Ortega in Nicaragua, Raúl Castro in Cuba, Hipólito Mejía in the Dominican Republic, Andrés Manuel López Obrador in Mexico, Mauricio Funes and Nayib Bukele in El Salvador).

Table 4 The rise of gender identity laws and ruling party ideology

Left	Center Left	Center Right
Bolivia: Morales (2016)	Panama: Torrijos (2006)	Peru: Kuczynski (2016)
Ecuador: Correa (2016)	Uruguay: Vázquez (2009)	Mexico*: Peña Nieto (2017)
	Argentina: Kirchner (2012)	Brazil: Temer (2018)
	Colombia: Santos (2015)	Chile: Piñera (2018)

Notes: *Reduced restrictions for voting.
In some countries, trans status can lead to vote suppression. Trans individuals with non-updated ID cards may not want to vote if voting centers check IDs or divide lines according to gender (www.reuters.com/article/us-ecuador-election-transgender/ecuador-transgender-people-vote-for-first-time-according-to-chosen-gender-idUSKBN15Y0SN; https://acepro ject.org/electoral-advice/archive/questions/replies/186593731#460868610).
Source: Muñoz-Pogossian (2020).

Another problem with the ruling-party-ideology hypothesis has to do with trans rights. In general, the advancement on trans rights has been limited, but the one area where progress has occurred – identity rights – emerged under both left-wing and right-wing parties (Choi et al. 2020, Muñoz-Pogossian 2020). Many of these rights, incidentally, came by way of legislation.

It is worth adding a final word about center-right parties and LGBTQ movements. In some European countries, center-right parties have embraced parts of the LGBTQ agenda and even candidates (Reynolds 2020). In Latin America, in contrast, the connections between center-right parties and LGBTQ causes are far more limited and probably shrinking. This carries a cost. It is harder for LGBTQ movements to lobby more conservative groups, especially the private sector, without these ties to center-right parties. The weak and weakening ties between LGBTQ groups and center-right parties, however, might explain the rise of an unusual type of organization in many Latin American countries: LGBTQ chambers of commerce. These chambers are rare in the Global South, but they have emerged and stayed fairly active in Argentina, Brazil, Colombia, the Dominican Republic, Ecuador, Mexico, and Uruguay. Although at times these chambers are the subject of criticism by both leftist LGBTQ groups and conservative groups, these chambers have succeeded in working with the private sector and the public sector to promote diversity within their staff, services, and client base.[19] These chambers help offset the negative effects of weak ties between LGBT groups and center-right parties.

---

[19] There is growing evidence that the size of the "LGBTQ economy" in the region is important, and this encourages the activities of these chambers. In 2018, the LGBTQ economy of the region was

A related hypothesis to the role of ruling parties has to do with presidential leadership. The hard-to-crack research question is whether presidential interventions are independent rather than dependent variables and whether they are decisive.

No one disputes that there can be no stronger force than a president pushing for an LGBTQ cause. Latin America offers examples of strong presidential commitments but also equivocation, even on the part of the same president. Several examples of presidential commitments include: the famous (and very-last-minute) decision by Argentine president Cristina Fernández de Kirchner to support marriage equality, which immediately prompted her party to vote along the same lines in congress; the full support by Uruguayan president José Mujica for same-sex marriage and the decision by Costa Rican president Luis Guillermo Solís to go to international courts in order to get support on behalf of moving forward with LGBTQ rights, and his successor, Carlos Alvarado, to encourage adoption of the international ruling; Colombian president Juan Manuel Santos's willingness to include LGBTQ themes in Peace Accords; the last-minute decision by Rafael Correa in Ecuador to support a gender-identity law.

It's clear that these cases of presidential intervention moved things along. The question is whether what needs to be explained is their effect (presidential intervention as an independent variable) or the factors that prompted presidents to embrace the cause (presidential intervention as a dependent variable). Most scholars agree that all presidential interventions occurred on the heels of long-standing pressure by either social movements acting on their own and displaying visibility (measured in terms of strength of gay pride) (Kollman and Sagarzazu 2017), or in collaboration with other actors such as bureaucrats and other public officials. There is also the role of external pressure (either in terms of strength of global connection or examples from neighboring countries (Kollman and Sagarzazu 2017).

The other question has to do with counterfactual: had there not been presidential intervention, would change have happened? Presidents tend to help with legislative victories, but some of the most important victories have come by way of courts, where courts have often acted independently of presidents. The role of courts thus requires more attention.

6.4 Courts

More so than ruling parties, it has been courts in the region have emerged as the most important force advancing LGBTQ rights (Lester 2012, Pierceson 2013,

---

estimated to account for US$253 billion, representing, in some cases, up to 5 percent of a country's GDP (Pérez Díaz 2018).

Encarnación 2014). Courts have done more than issue legally-binding rulings. They have also offered "guidance" to the legislative branch to reorder messy and inconsistent civil codes, and advised other branches of government on best practices to interact with the LGBTQ community, strengthen human rights through stronger interpretations of both local and international human rights standards, and settle differences in the way that subnational actors interpret LGBTQ ordinances and legislations (Campana and Vaggione 2021). It seems that for courts to be receptive and active on behalf of LGBTQ rights, they need to exhibit at least three characteristics:

(a) Sufficient assertiveness, and maybe independence. The former conveys a certain degree of professionalism; the latter, a certain degree of ability to go against the preferences of the other branches of government.
(b) Progressivism. The courts must subscribe to a theory of jurisprudence that is amenable to a progressive agenda – meaning, sympathetic to issues of human rights, equality before the law, antidiscrimination, reproductive and women's rights, commitment to separation of state and church, etc.
(c) Transnational legalism. This involves at least two dimensions (see Halliday and Shaffer 2015). First, transnational legalism is the idea that international treaties take priority over national law. Second, judges and litigants can invoke legal cases from abroad to make legal claims.

If we combine these variables – assertiveness and progressiveness/transnationalism – a 2x2 matrix can be generated to explain the role of courts in the advancements of LGBTQ rights as in Table 5. Cells represent predicted outcomes in terms of position vis-à-vis LGBTQ rights and specifically same-sex marriage, each with examples. The idea is that the most assertive and progressive/transnational courts produce the strongest LGBTQ rulings. The rest produce softer rulings, no rulings, or even unsympathetic rulings.

Transnational legalism, incidentally, has emerged as an important element in explaining the LGBTQ rights transformation in Latin America. In Argentina, for example, when the LGBTQ community began to advocate on behalf of LGBTQ rights, they often invoked legal cases from other countries, especially Spain. In Chile, the state was forced to address a famous case of lesbian parenting discrimination ("Atala Riffo and daughters versus Chile") after the Inter-American Court of Human Rights found the Chilean state to be in violation of the American Convention of Human Rights. In Costa Rica, the constitution explicitly states that international rulings, especially on human rights, take precedence over national law. So when the Inter-American Court of Human Rights declared in 2018 that signatories must offer to LGBTQ citizens all rights, including marriage rights, the Costa Rican court complied.

Table 5 Court features and LGBTQ rights, 2003–2013

	Assertive/independent courts	**Nonassertive/beholden courts**
Progressive/ transnational	Strong pro-LGBTQ rulings: Courts likely to promote more comprehensive LGBTQ rights or block serious homophobic initiatives. (Brazil, Colombia, Ecuador (after 2017)**, Argentina*, Uruguay, Costa Rica)	Soft rulings: Courts likely to advance *limited* rights such as nondiscrimination norms, if at all. (Argentina*, Mexico, Ecuador**, Bolivia, Nicaragua)
Nonprogressive	Hesitant courts (Chile, Peru***)	Unsympathetic courts (Venezuela, Dominican Republic, Guatemala, Paraguay, Honduras)

Notes:

* Argentina in this period is probably an in-between case in terms of assertiveness and progressivism. That explains why the Courts did not play a proactive or consistently supportive role in gay rights, but they have also not been major obstacles either.

** Ecuador's supreme court became more independent after the end of the Correa administration in 2017.

*** Peru is probably an in-between case in terms of assertiveness (Basabe-Serrano 2014).

Source: Author from Corrales (2017).

The remarkable aspect of courts and LGBTQ rights is that, contrary to the historic role of courts in Latin America, courts have been able to take positions that defy the preferences not just of public opinion, but also important actors across society and in government, including popular presidents. Having said that, courts do not become gay champions out of the blue. Many times, their rulings are the result of carefully crafted legal pressure and strategic choices by social movements (Campana and Vaggione 2021), suggesting that even in this realm, institution-movement interaction is at work.

Scholars have also pointed out drawbacks to relying on court rulings to advance LGBTQ rights in general (not just Latin America), the so-called, judicialization of LGBTQ politics. One is that the court rulings focus mostly on legal and regulatory change, prompting some to question whether they are enough to truly tackle more structural forms of homophobia and transphobia and may even lead to a false sense of triumphalism (Figari 2010, Kapur 2018). Second, court rulings may have helped fuel a backlash against LGBTQ rights because they often lead to the impression that decisions are being made by elites, imposing narrow preferences over the rest of society (more later).

6.5 Federalism

Federalism has been a mixed blessing for LGBTQ rights. On the one hand, federalism has been one avenue rights have advanced when the national system is closed. The countries with the most advanced forms of federalism – Argentina, Brazil, and Mexico – were the first to start making progress on same-sex marriage precisely because advocates could relocate their struggles to subnational levels when they found stiff barrier at the national level. Advocates were able to discern which subnational units were more amenable to change, and targeted those places – that is, LGBTQ movements were strategic (Schulenberg 2013, Encarnación 2015, Kollman and Sagarzazu 2017, López 2017, 2018). A similar type of strategic targeting was followed in the United States. In addition, in Mexico, federalism has allowed local legislatures to play a more prominent role. Among the nineteen entities in Mexico that grant same-sex marriage (eighteen states and the City of Mexico), eleven came about via legislative statutes.

But federalism creates problems. It can result in a bizarre form of diversity of rights that contradicts the notion of equality before the law. Some states end up granting rights; others do not. In part, these gaps can occur because federalism also provides room for conservative forces, which can actually be far stronger at the subnational level than progressive forces and institutions. Federalism can thus "slow down and hinder" nationwide progress toward LGBTQ rights (López 2017).

In Argentina and Brazil, this variation in inequality before the law produced by federalism was solved with a congressional law in the former (the famous 2010 law legalizing gay marriage, which was the first such law in Latin America and the second in the Americas after Canada) and through a court ruling in the latter. In Mexico, there has not been a national directive other than a court order that all states must recognize same-sex marriages performed in other states.

6.6 Unity

There is almost unanimous consensus that internal unity is key for any social movement to have influence in politics. While the LGBTQ movement has always been prone to internal divisions due to intersectionalities and disagreements about priorities and strategies to address patriarchy and heteronormativity (Brown

2002, Somma et al. 2019), it has nonetheless managed to come together in a number of key policy battles. Achieving unity behind any given policy battle is crucial.

For the sake of space, I will skip discussing how LGBTQ movements in Latin America have overcome previous divisions in earlier battles, in order to focus on more recent potential fissure within the movement: the extent to which the rise of trans demands may be testing the movement's ability to maintain unity.

The rise of the trans movement has helped diversify the political agenda of the LGBTQ, but it has also produced some tensions within the movement. Because scholars recognize that a unified movement is essential, it is important to explore whether potential divisions stemming from the trans revolution might impair future progress.

It should be said at the outset that talk of divisions can be overstated. In most counties, most LGB activists are in favor of, and, in fact, fully embrace most of the demands from the trans community. However, some rifts exist.

For instance, one of the key demands of the trans community has been to end the gay male dominance of the LGBTQ movement, what some people deem a type of homonormativity (Carvalho and Carrara 2013, RedLacTrans 2019). Gay male dominance is a reflection of patriarchy, the legacy of the AIDS crisis, and maybe even class. During the AIDS crisis, international organizations privileged providing support to affected groups, and one such group was the so-called "men who have sex with men" (MSM) demographic. This gave rise to the rise of men as leaders of many LGBTQ organizations, with international support. Trans activists, many of whom come from low-income sectors, feel that the preference for male leaders in the LGBTQ community is also a reflection of aporohobia, and a preference for the middle and upper class (Carvalho and Carrara 2013). Along with lesbians, bisexuals, and nonbinary people, trans activists have long argued that this dominance of gay men in the LGBTQ movement needs to be balanced, and this has produced internal clashes.

Scholars have also established that an important ingredient in LGBTQ victories has been the ability of the LGBTQ movement to form alliances with stronger, larger social movements, especially feminists and human rights advocates (Díez 2015, Encarnación 2015). The trans movement is also testing some of these alliances. A conflict that has become salient in the last decade involves trans women and some strands of feminism and human rights advocates over not just what it means to be a real woman (Iricibar 2019), but also the admissibility of sex work (Daich 2012).

On the one hand, most trans theorists believe that their movement is comfortably ensconced in feminism, and in fact, represents an improvement on contemporary feminism. Like many feminists, trans women and men feel discriminated or misunderstood by men, whether heterosexual or homosexual (Carvalho and Carrara 2013). Trans people share many worldviews with feminists: sex does not make a person, individuals have exclusive rights over their bodies, patriarchal disdain and invisibilization are pervasive, gender roles are constructs that are often imposed, and diversity construed broadly (to include race, gender, class, ethnicity, and education levels) is a political asset and collective good (De Jesus and Alves 2012, Kaas 2016, Garza 2018, Garriga-López 2019). In addition, contemporary feminist and trans theorists have been at the forefront of awareness-raising of all forms of gender-based violence, physical as well as mental. There is an argument to be made that in a region where violence is high and (lesbo)femicide is on the rise and relatively tolerated (see Joseph 2017, ECLAC 2020), violence against trans people is also likely to be rampant.[20]

Despite these common positions and agendas, now known as "transfeminism," some strands of feminism in Latin America, as in the North Atlantic, see the trans movement with suspicion. They often see trans women as individuals who at some point enjoyed male privilege, and are therefore less complete as women, and trans men as individuals who assimilate rather than resist patriarchy (see De Jesus and Alves 2012, Chávez 2016).[21] Many times, these specific feminists want a return to identification based on sex rather than gender identity (Lecuona 2020), a stand that places them on the same camp as some conservative religious figures (more later). Some cis gay males have been known to be equally suspicious (Kaas 2016).

Trans activists of course resent these arguments, and retort that non-trans feminists have enjoyed cis privileges and that does not make them any less victims of the patriarchy and therefore less complete. They also retort with an anti-colonial claim: the trans condition and two-spiritedness could be

---

[20] In 2018, the Latin American countries with the highest rate of femicide per 100,000 women were: El Salvador (6.8), Honduras (5.1), Bolivia (2.3), Guatemala (2.0) and the Dominican Republic (1.9) (Galindo and Gaytan 2019). Lesbians have been able to elevate cases of lesbicide to national attention to raise awareness about lesbofemicide (e.g., Pepa Gaitán, murdered in Argentina in 2010; Mónica Briones and Nicole Saavedra, murdered in Chile in 1984 and 2016, respectively; Marielle Franco, murdered in Brazil in 2018) (see DW 2020).

[21] Another polemic involving trans men, in Brazil at least, has to do with surgery. Some trans men in Brazil decide to undergo surgery and then choose "to pass" as physically male with a cis identity. The decision to pass as cis creates controversies across the entire trans community (Almeida 2012). In addition, trans women in Brazil complain that trans men can obtain changes in their legal documents without undergoing surgery, whereas trans women can only change their documents after undergoing surgery, a procedure that is risky and some even say mutilatory (de Jesus and Alves 2012).

considered a form of "reclaiming indigenous worldviews stolen from us through hundreds of years of colonization" (Chávez 2016:63).

Another division with feminists and human rights advocates relates to sex work (Garriga-López 2019). Many Latin American trans women engage in sex work. Almost half of transgender women in San Salvador, for instance, report that their main income is sex work (AVERT 2019). Some trans people in Latin America engage in sex work because of lack of choice: there are way too many barriers in the education and formal employment sector for trans women to flourish (Johnson et al. 2020). Others do it because they want to: it is an arena where they feel desired rather than repudiated. Whatever the reasons, a frequent demand of many trans women is to join forces with groups advocating for the rights of sex workers (Cabezas 2019). This position has clashed with "abolitionist feminists" – those who feel that sex work should never be legalized or promoted (Piscitelli 2014).

Having said that, as real as these fissures are, they have not been serious enough to weaken the LGBTQ movement or the greater ties uniting this community. Trans activism in Latin America has overall given the LGBTQ movement more power, more diversity, and a broader scope of themes to focus on. As Guy (2010) suggests, despite differences, gay and even trans men are far more able to bridge divides between men and women than cis straight men, making the movement amenable to powerful alliances with feminist movements.

7 LGBTQ Rights v. Abortion Rights

One lingering puzzle in LGBTQ and sexuality politics in Latin America is why the region has been able to enact pro-LGBTQ laws and policies while at the same time remaining so restrictive on abortion rights. There is no one theory that can fully explain this puzzle, but some compelling arguments have been offered.

First, the puzzle. Table 6 shows the levels of restrictions on abortion rights in the region as of early 2021. The number of cells with NO is far greater for abortion rights than for LGBTQ rights (Table 6).[22] The most liberal position on abortion rights is abortion on demand: any pregnant woman demanding an abortion is entitled to one. Only three countries offer that right: Uruguay, Cuba, and Argentina. In the case of Argentina, the right was established only in 2021, eleven years after the approval of same-sex marriage. The rest of Latin America offers abortions based on conditions, if at all. Those conditions require

---

[22] In September 2021, the Mexican supreme court approved abortion rights nationwide. It ruled unconstitutional a law in the state of Coahuila criminalizing women who undergo abortions or people who aid them. The ruling is binding in all states. Prior to this ruling, only four of Mexico's 32 federal entities offered abortion rights (Oaxaca, Veracruz, Hidalgo and Mexico City). Perhaps not coincidentally, the ruling occurred shortly after the the the state of Texas began implementing a law that effectively bans abortions after six weeks.

Table 6 Abortion rights in Latin America in 2020: When is abortion allowed?

Countries	To save mother's life	To preserve the mother's physical health	If fetal impairment	In case of rape	In case of incest	To preserve pyschological health	Socioeconomic reasons	By petition from mother	With parental authorization
Cuba	Yes	Yes	Yes	Yes	Yes	Yes	Yes	Yes	Yes
Uruguay	Yes	Yes	Yes	Yes	Yes	Yes	Yes	Yes	Yes*
Argentina	Yes	Yes	Yes	Yes	Yes	Yes	Yes	Yes	Yes
Mexico	Partial***	Partial***	Partial***	Partial***	No	Partial****	Partial***	Partial***	Partial***
Bolivia	Yes	Yes	No	Yes	Yes	Yes	No	No	No
Colombia	Yes	Yes	Yes	Yes	Yes	No	No	No	No
Panama	Yes	Yes	Yes	Yes	No	No	No	No	No
Chile	Yes	No	Yes	Yes	No	No	No	No	No
Brazil	Yes	No	No**	Yes	No	No	No	No	No
Costa Rica	Yes	Yes	No	No	No	No	No	No	No
Ecuador	Yes	Yes	No	No****	No	No	No	No	No
Venezuela	Yes	No	No	No	No	No	No	No	No
Paraguay	Yes	No	No	No	No	No	No	No	No
Guatemala	Yes	No	No	No	No	No	No	No	No
Dom. Rep.	No	No	No	No	No	No	No	No	No
El Salvador	No	No	No	No	No	No	No	No	No
Honduras	No	No	No	No	No	No	No	No	No
Nicaragua	No	No	No	No	No	No	No	No	No

Notes:

* For women under 18, however women can present medical information to judge who may then wave parental consent.

** In case of anencephaly, abortion is allowed.

*** A bill legalizing abortion was submitted to congress by the president in 2020.

**** Legal on a state-by-state basis.

***** Legal when a person with a mental disability is pregnant from rape.

Sources: See Appendix.

other actors, such as a medical professional, sometimes even a judge, to weigh in. These conditions make Latin America the most restrictive region in the world when it comes to abortion rights (Singh et al. 2018, Center for Reproductive Rights 2020, Marcus-Delgado 2020).

The easiest cases to explain are perhaps Cuba and Uruguay. These cases conform to the religious opening hypothesis: the influence of the church was low at the time the policy was set in place. Cuba decriminalized abortion in 1965, when the communist regime had finally decimated the Catholic Church (Holbrook 2010). In addition, in Cuba, as in many communist countries, the state has always been interested in controlling population growth, so abortion was adopted for both progressive reasons (as a women's right) but also autocratic reasons (family control). In Uruguay, the policy was enacted in 2012, at a point when church attendance levels were at a very low point, and Evangelicalism was still very minor. The change was driven by feminist forces and their allies (Wood et al. 2016).

The most complex puzzles are Argentina, Brazil, Colombia, Mexico, Chile, Ecuador, and even Costa Rica. Argentina is puzzling because abortion rights came long after LGBTQ rights and following very intense political battles. The other cases also exhibit the most pro-LGBTQ rights in the region and yet their abortion rights remain limited.

If the explanation for lack of abortion rights in those countries is religious influence, why were they able to expand LGBTQ rights as much as they did? Both agendas have been opposed by the same religious actors (Fernández-Anderson 2020). By the same token, these cases also defy most of the political institutions hypotheses discussed. If institutions made possible their LGBTQ rights, why have they failed to liberalize abortion rights?

It may very well be that we must go beyond religion and institutions to explain this puzzle and focus on other factors, such as differences across constituencies, or more specifically, differences in terms of the closet, class structures, internal divisions, and messaging by opponents.

The closet difference has to do with the fact that for pregnant women interested in terminating their pregnancy, an underground abortion is available and easy to hide. Latin America is the region in the world that performs the highest number of abortions, it's just that these abortions are underground (Singh et al. 2018). The prevalence of underground abortions means that there is a closet for aborting mothers, just as there is for LGBTQ people. The difference between both closet options is that perhaps the closet has become less comfortable for a number of LGBTQ people than the closet option for women terminating their pregnancy. Increases in coming out experiences in the LGBTQ community lead to greater social contacts and thus greater social acceptance (Dion and Díez 2020). Many times, women who get an underground abortion find it easy to hide the secret. Often, their relatives support them in keeping the secret.

Another argument, strongly made by Htun (2003, 2009), focuses on class divide. In Latin America, upper-income groups are less impacted by the negative effects of the abortion closet, and, thus, have less incentive to end it. They have access to *safe* underground abortions. The pro-choice movement, therefore, has trouble enlisting large-enough sectors of the class with the most bargaining leverage – high-income elites.

Perhaps the key difference has to do with the unity of each movement's core constituency. Despite divisions across LGBTQ groups, most of the political causes embraced by them tend to unite their constituents: the fight against discrimination and hate crimes, the struggle for recognition and respect, and the expansion of rights. Even the question of same-sex marriage, which at the very beginning was very divisive in the LGBTQ community, over time became a topic that most members of the LGBTQ community decided to embrace (as a right to have though not necessarily as a right to exercise). In contrast, the pro-choice position divides the key constituency of this movement: women (Htun 2003). This division in the core constituency of potential beneficiaries of this policy lessens the movement's bargaining leverage.

A related argument may have to do with preference rankings. Women may have decided that other women's rights are more important – such as broader human rights, divorce protections, welfare programs for mothers, and even political quotas for women (Morgan 2015). This contrasts sharply with the same-sex movement in Latin America. While initially many LGBTQ people saw same-sex marriage as a lower priority, in the mid 2000s, perhaps following international examples, the movement converged to make same-sex marriage a priority.

Yet another reason could be the role of men, or the lack of support by men. The LGBTQ movement, for good or evil, has been historically led by men, and, in a patriarchal society, that counts for something. It grants gravitas. In contrast, the abortion rights movement is led by women. Although more men are supporting abortion rights in Latin America than ever, as a collective, men have been "remarkably passive" (Molyneux 2017) on a number of gender causes, not just abortion rights. Many feminist causes don't enjoy the unfortunate "male privilege" that carries so much weight in patriarchal societies.

Finally, the messaging by the pro-life group is formidable and difficult to challenge. While the LGBTQ movement in Latin America has found effective forms of issue-framing, linking their movement to sympathetic ideals shared by large sectors of the population, such as human rights (Longaker and Haider-Markel 2014, Encarnación 2015, 2018, Somma et al. 2019), in the abortion debate, it is the conservative side that often has the upper hand with framing.

Pro-life groups have been able to make the point that abortion, at any point, is tantamount to killing an innocent person. The use of the words killing, innocent, and person is deliberate, intended to produce moral repulsion. It is also a framing that is intended to sway even health professionals, most of whom profess to be in the service of saving (not killing) human life. Furthermore, Catholic leaders have been able to frame their pro-life position to fit nicely into the "human rights framework" that is so well received in Latin America today, by arguing that they are defending the human rights of the unborn (Morgan 2014). While the Catholic Church has become less intolerant of other "sins," it remains stringent on the issue of abortion (Kane 2008, Corrales and Sagarzazu 2019).

The case of Argentina deserves special mention. After so many tries, the country was able to approve abortion rights in December 2020. What changed? It could very well be that the power balance turned in favor of pro-choice social movements, as was the case with LGBTQ rights in the late 2000s. Fernández-Anderson (2018, 2020) argues that a new balance of forces between the Church and feminist movements preceded the change. The Church's resistance in Argentina softened while the feminist movement has "grown exponentially." The pro-choice movement in Argentina represents more than 550 organizations across all provinces and has the support of different professions and sectors of society.

In addition, it could very well be that feminist movements in Argentina, which at one point served as inspiration to the LGBTQ movement, drew some inspiration from the LGBTQ movement in their final drive for abortion rights. Specifically, women's movements succeeded in bridging ideological and class divides: they canvassed poor neighborhoods to make less-affluent women feel empowered to demand change, and they carried out campaigns targeting conservative middle-class women to recognize the double standard of publicly appearing antiabortion while privately acting pro-choice (Corrales 2018). They popularized the view that "the rich abort, the poor die." That way, woman's movements framed abortion as an issue of social justice and public health – rather than the United States' framing, in which it is an individual right (Daby and Moseley 2020). They have also framed the decision to abort as an instance of empowerment–the moment in which the women finally takes control of her life about which it should feel no shame–which parallels how LGBTQ movements frame the process of coming out (see Morcillo and Felitti 2017).

8 The Current Backlash: Late 2010s to the Present

After so much progress on LGBTQ rights and policies, the region may have entered into a backlash period: opponents of LGBTQ rights seem to be acquiring new tools to contain or even roll back pro-LGBTQ gains (López Pacheco 2018, Corrales 2020a). What are the elements of this backlash?

First, the electorate has changed. As LGBTQ issues become more salient in public discourse and policy change, a cleavage on sexuality, that might have been dormant in the electorate, may have become more salient. While more news coverage of LGBTQ stories and policies may prompt more voters to become openly supportive politically mobilized, and treat LGBTQ issues as priorities when deciding how to vote (de Abreu Maia et al. 2020, Ayoub and Page 2020), other voters may come out as homophobic and become political about it as well (Smith and Boas 2020). Education, incidentally, seems to matter in shaping this new cleavage: the expansion of tolerance tends to be stronger among more educated Latin Americans than less educated ones and among younger people (Chaux et al. 2021, Navarro et al. 2019, de Abreu Maia et al. 2020), except among Evangelicals, where homophobic attitudes prevail regardless of levels of education or even age group (Corrales and Sagarzazu 2019, Chaux et al. 2021).

Second, LGBTQ activism has triggered a major change in religious alliances. The competition between Catholic and Evangelical clergies that dominated Latin America's religious scene since the 1970s is morphing into increasing cooperation (Corrales 2020a). The aim of this cooperation is to join forces to fight the growing influence of secular and irreligious organizations and voters. Together with lay politicians, Catholic and Evangelical clergies are joining efforts to stop further progress and push back on some gains. In the late 2010s, anti-LGBTQ candidates came close to reaching the presidency in Costa Rica, Colombia, and Chile, and they have been recognized members of ruling coalitions in Brazil, Mexico, Bolivia, Honduras, Paraguay, and Guatemala.

Third, the resistance to LGBTQ rights has acquired a new framing mechanism that is potentially more palatable for more secular societies or populist movements than the frames used to block marriage rights. The new frame is opposition to what has been baptized as "ideology of gender" (CBMW 2017, Vela Barba 2017, Vatican City 2019). This is a term designed to label any effort to promote acceptance of sexual fluidity, which, by extension, includes all LGBTQ issues. The key idea is that the pro-LGBTQ agenda is promoting an anti-biblical ideology rejecting the fact that all humans are born with a basic binary anatomical distinction, namely, male and female; that gender identity must always conform to that anatomy; and that a sexual relationship can only exist between the sexes/genders and not within the same sex/gender. The key word in this new frame is "ideology." By stressing that a pro-LGBTQ agenda is an ideology or belief, they are insinuating that it is not a scientific proposition, and therefore, adults have the right to protect themselves and, more important, their children from exposure to it. In Brazil, for instance, a bill to stop sexual education in public schools is titled "No-Party School," to suggest that teaching these topics is an effort to impose a party ideology (Reis Brandão and Cabral 2019). Ideology of gender thus reinvokes classic theories of "child protectionism" that have been used to support homo- and transphobic stands in the past. In Latin America, the preferred slogan has been *Con mis hijos no te metas* ("Don't mess with my kids").

As the politics of LGBTQ rights expansion moves away from partnership discussions and more toward youth-related themes such as gay parenting, multiparenting, teacher training, anti-bullying campaigns, school education, etc., homophobic groups can once again invoke the child-protection and family-autonomy right to cast their opposition to these policies. The concept of ideology of gender has thus given homophobes a way to reframe their position in terms of rights: the rights of family, the rights of children, the rights of religious people. This allows them to cast their arguments in secular even liberal-democratic terms, which allows them to unite conservative Christians across denominations with secular forces. Scholars have tried to point out nonetheless the illiberal foundations of this frame. This frame, for instance, has converted "family rights" as "more significant than individual rights" (Biroli and Caminotti 2020). In addition, this frame embraces an illiberal idea famously articulated by Rafael Correa that feminism is divided between a commonsense version "that we can all support" and a radical version that is self-serving (Garriga-López 2016). Despite these normative criticques, the new frame grants supporters the opportunity to claim that they are taking the side of the good kind of feminism, and thus protect themselves from accusations of being anti-feminist (Rodríguez-Rondón and Rivera-Amarillo 2020).

Another element about the movement against gender ideology is its trans-nationalism (Faur and Viveros Vigoya 2020). The movement against gender ideology was born outside Latin America, in response to major inroads by women's groups in United Nations conferences worldwide in the mid-1990s. It was initially fostered by Catholic clergies worldwide, now in alliance with Evangelical clergies, but also by many right-wing populists outside Europe, looking for arguments against progressives and defenders of human rights, and always suspicious of intellectualism and diversity more generally (Fassin 2020).

One way to visualize the impact that the ideology of gender backlash is having on politics is to focus on the 2016 Colombian Peace Accords and how the final version was changed to accommodate these conservative forces. The final draft of the Accords became famous worldwide, among several reasons, because it had a strong focus on gender and was also the first peace accord to explicitly recognize LGBTQ victims. Supporters of the movement against gender ideology mobilized in 2016 to defeat the final draft in a referendum. Following the defeat, the government was forced to rewrite the accords. The second version reduced the number of times the word gender was used, in favor of woman, and deleted entirely references to sexual orientation (see

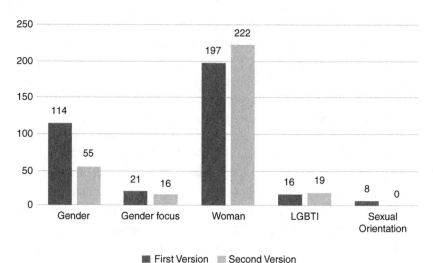

Figure 3 Word usage in Colombia's Peace Accord, first versus second versions

Notes: First version: September 2016. Second version: November 2016.

Source: Cossette and Saba Perez (2019).

Figure 3) (Cossette and Saba Perez 2019). This transnationalism makes it harder for local actors to contain it on their own.

Finally, the backlash represents a return to the past – potentially back to the nineteenth century. The rise of LGBTQ rights might have made religion once again a major political cleavage in the region, as it was during most the nineteenth century. Groups organized by religious leaders are now questioning the concept of laicism. They are eager to confront secularists, anticlericals, and light Catholics by supporting candidates and causes that are overtly pro-religion. While religion never ceased to be important in Latin American politics, always defining key cleavages – conservatives versus anticlericals in the nineteenth century (J. E. W. 1966), Christian Democrats versus secularists and social-democrats in the early to mid twentieth century (Vasconi et al. 1993), semi-Marxist Catholics versus conservatives until the 1970s (Lowy and Pompan 1993) – religious groups in Latin America had come to grudgingly accept the notion of a secular state by the 1960s. The rise of LGBTQ politics in Latin America has ended that impasse. Evangelicals are now eager to conquer politics (Pérez Guadalupe and Grundberger 2017; Zilla 2018). And they do so by openly protesting public policies pertaining to education; mobilizing street and online protests by lay people (*marchas por la vida*); supporting candidates for office who cater to their preferences; and, especially among Evangelicals, even running for office (as mayors, legislators, and even presidents) by explicitly flaunting their pro-religion policy preferences.

A look at the Jair Bolsonaro and Miguel Díaz-Canel administrations in Brazil and Cuba provides a glimpse of the potential political impact on LGBTQ progress that could come when this backlash comes close to power. Bolsonaro ran for office with an explicit anti-left platform (Hunter and Power 2019), which included a strong anti-LGBTQ discourse and an open alliance with Evangelical leaders. Once in office, he did not waste time rolling back pro-LGBTQ policies. In August 2019, for instance, Bolsonaro announced that he would discontinue funding movies with LGBTQ themes, arguing that such funding (approximately US$17.4 million) was like "throwing money away." In December 2019, Bolsonaro decided not to renew the license for TV Escola, a public-funded TV channel, for promoting leftist ideas and gender ideology. In Cuba, Díaz-Canel yielded to pressure from 21 Evangelical churches to scrap the government's plan to introduce same-sex marriage in the new 2019 constitution, and subsequentely, repressed LGBTQ protesters.

Sometimes, state-directed homo- and transphobia are less intentional, but just as severe. In Venezuela, Maduro's decision to restrict the use of hard currency to acquire imports, including medicine for HIV patients, has caused a resurgence of AIDS death rates. In Central America, the states' failure to contain crime continues to take a toll on the LGBTQ community. For all these reasons, despite legal gains, Latin America continues to produce significant *"sexilios,"* a term coined to describe migration based on conditions of sexuality (La Fountain-Stokes 2004, Martinez-Reyes 2018, Mathema 2018, Mogrovejo 2018).

Historically, Latin American sexiles have migrated mostly to the United States, Canada, and European countries. In the case of the United States, nearly 4,400 openly LGBTQ people, mostly from Central America, sought asylum between 2007 and 2017 (Almendral and Villasana 2021). Now, sexiles are starting to go to other Latin American countries. Sexiles may find legal protections abroad, but not always welcoming attitudes, with locals often responding with a mixture of nativism and aporophobia, not just homo- and transphobia. The pandemic of course has created barriers for migrants, and has often left them stranded in passage countries, often without legal protections. The first LGBTQ Migration Center in Latin America was created in Manaus, Brazil, to help Venezuelans cope with these challenges (Su and Valiquette 2020). For a while, Brazil was a favorite destination for LGBTQ refugees from Latin America for its legal protections (Lopez 2018). But now, in the Bolsonaro era, Brazil is producing its own sexiles. The most famous recent example is Jean Wyllys, Brazil's first and only openly gay congressman, who resigned his post and left the Brazil in 2019 after receiving death threats.

Not much research has been conducted on the cost of sexile on sending countries. One exception is Crehan et al.'s 2021 study on the non-Spanish-speaking Caribbean. Inspired by the pathbreaking work by Badgett et al. (2019),

Crehan et al. found that a significant portion of sexiles includes people with high skills and high education, producing a costly brain and workforce drain for sending countries.

Although this Element has focused on the clash with religious authorities, and to a lesser extent, state actors that are unresponsive or even antagonistic to LGBTQ demands, it is important to stress that ultimately the backlash against LGBTQ rights is predicated on lingering societal attitudes. Even where rights have expanded, ministries have become respectful, or religious authorities have become less condemnatory, societal discrimination persists. This discrimination, quite often, is most intense close to home. LGBTQ youth continue to report that some of the most direct and virulent forms of discrimination occur at home.

The prevalence of societal discrimination can be, shockingly, still strong in countries that have advanced the most legally. A recent survey from Colombia, for instance, reveals that one in five LGBTQ respondents had received conversion therapy; three out of four were bullied at least once before turning eighteen; and one in four had attempted suicide at least once (Choi et al. 2020). Especially problematic is the persistence of homo- and transphobia in schools. In Argentina, perhaps Latin America's most important LGBTQ legal champion, more than 66 percent of LGBTQ students report hearing homo- and transphobic comments from school faculty and staff (similar responses are reported in Mexico, Colombia, and Peru; a bit less in Uruguay and Chile) (Kosciw and Zongrone 2019). LGBTQ students feel so unsafe at schools that they often avoid spaces such as bathrooms (Kosciw and Zongrone 2019).

Furthermore, there are signs that greater visibility of LGBTQ people has also produced an expansion of hate crimes. In Honduras, for instance, the average homicide rate of LGBTQ individuals went from 1.4 deaths per year between 1994 and 2008 to nearly 30 per year after 2009 (see Figure 4) (Bleir and Smith 2019). While other factors might explain this increase, it is impossible to rule out a connection between this spike and greater visibility of LGBTQ groups.

That said, two countertrends may help contain this current backlash. Most studies show that tolerance is increasing over time and that the younger generations are typically more accepting of LGBTQ rights (see Table 7).

Research is emerging indicating that access to information, in the form of more education, more internet usage, and even more exposure to LGBTQ people also produces more acceptance (Dion and Díez 2017, 2020, Díez and Dion 2018). One caveat is that these "modernization-type" factors moving in the direction of greater acceptance seem to make little difference among Evangelicals (Corrales and Sagarzazu 2019).

Table 7 Percentage who say homosexuality should be accepted by society, by age group

	Total population		By age group in 2019		
	2002	2019	18–29	30–49	50+
Argentina	66	76	85	76	70
Brazil	61*	67	82	67	59
Mexico	54	69	77	72	53

Notes: * Data taken in 2011.
Source: Poushter and Kent (2020).

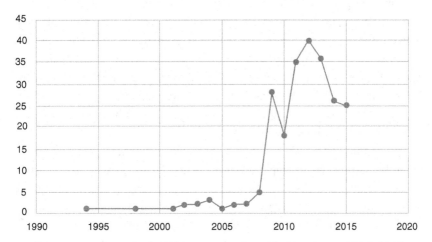

Figure 4 Murders of LGBTQ persons reported in Honduras, 1994–2015.
Source: Bleir and Smith (2019).

Second, there is finally some evidence demonstrating that legal changes have a positive effect on public opinion. In countries where legislatures and courts expand LGBTQ rights, the public responds by becoming even more favorable toward those policies (Chaux et al. 2021, de Abreu Maia et al. 2020). Changing policy even in the context of public opposition can actually help move public opinion toward greater acceptance.

Finally, it is important to mention the impact of the novel coronavirus pandemic on LGBTQ people (see Corrales 2020b). While many Latin American LGBTQ people are still struggling with the AIDS pandemic, the LGBTQ community had to confront a new pandemic that disproportionately impacts them. Four of the populations most severely affected by the pandemic in Latin America – informal workers, retail personnel, entertainment professionals, and people with preexisting health conditions – include a disproportionate number of

LGBTQ people. In addition, in Panama, Peru, and Colombia, authorities experimented with gender-based curfews ("*pico y género*"), which impacted trans people negatively. These gender curfews mandated men and women to be out on alternating days. This led to security guards and police targeting trans people for noncompliance, and even incidents of hate crimes. Trans activists were vocal in denouncing these lockdown measures and helping reverse them in Peru and Colombia.

9 Conclusion

The struggle for LGBTQ rights in Latin America is no longer in the closet. It is now an open and habitual theme in presidential debates, campaigns for national and local elections, discussions of public policies, pop culture, and household conversations. This coming out has generated profound transformations in most countries or, at least, in their larger cities. It has transformed laws, policies, and even attitudes in the direction of more acceptance and inclusion. Non-white, low-income LGBTQ Latin Americans have fewer opportunities to enjoy these rights, but at least institutional and discourse openings have been made for future generations to take advantage of.

This coming out has also produced a backlash. Conservative forces, perhaps taken by surprise by the rapid advances of the 2010s, have recouped. More fundamentally, the LGBTQ movement has triggered an unprecedented alliance between historic rivals: Catholic and Evangelical clergies. The call for twin tolerances in democracy famously made by Stepan (2000) – the state must not restrict freedom of worship, and religion must not restrict the policies of democratic state – is becoming a bit lopsided. Religious groups are receiving more tolerance than they are willing to offer in return. At the level of the electorate, the old pro- and anticlerical cleavage that dominated Latin American politics between Independence in the 1800s to the early Cold War in the 1950s might be making a comeback in the early twenty-first century. It is now comprised of irreligious and light Catholic voters on the one hand, and religious and church-attending voters on the other. At the level of party politics, the rise of this new religious lobbying and voting block is compelling previously secular center-right parties to become more conservative on issues of sexuality and less committed to laicity.

There is nonetheless some positive news for LGBTQ forces. These forces now constitute recognized and active social movements in almost every country of the region, with allies across society, parts of the bureaucracy, and the international scene. Younger generations and more educated Latin Americans are increasingly sympathetic to LGBTQ themes. LGBTQ forces have acquired a political presence, and, thus, power, that is hard to erase. They face domestic and international rivals, but they are able to resist. This can be seen from the experience with the Colombian peace accords. In the end, enemies of LGBTQ rights were unable to entirely erase references to LGBTQ terms. In fact, references to LGBTQ actually increased in the final draft. This could very well be a metaphor for the status of LGBTQ politics in 2020s: LGBTQ movements are facing long-standing discrimination and renewed forms attacks, but they have never been better equipped to fight back.

Appendix
Sources for abortion rights

Argentina:	www.aljazeera.com/news/2020/03/argentina-presi dent-introduce-bill-legalise-abortion-2003020 30410385.html
	www.amnesty.org/en/latest/news/2020/03/argentina-after-president-stands-by-his-word-to-legalise-abor tion/
	https://reproductiverights.org/worldabortionlaws? country=ARG&category[295]=295
Bolivia:	https://ipas.org/news/2017/December/legal-abor tion-access-greatly-expanded-in-bolivia
	https://reproductiverights.org/worldabortionlaws? country=BOL&category[295]=295
Brazil:	www.thelancet.com/journals/lanpub/article/ PIIS2468-2667(19)30204-X/fulltext
	www.hrw.org/legacy/women/abortion/brazil.html
	https://reproductiverights.org/worldabortionlaws? country=BRA&category[295]=295
Chile:	www.loc.gov/law/foreign-news/article/chile-law-permits-abortion-on-three-grounds/
	https://reproductiverights.org/worldabortionlaws? country=CHL&category[295]=295
Colombia:	www.guttmacher.org/fact-sheet/unintended-preg nancy-and-induced-abortion-colombia
	www.reproductiverights.org/press-room/10-years-of-legal-abortion-in-colombia
Costa Rica:	https://ticotimes.net/2019/12/11/costa-rica-takes-final-step-in-establishing-when-how-therapeutic-abortions-can-be-performed
	https://reproductiverights.org/worldabortionlaws? country=CRI&category[295]=295
	https://abortion-policies.srhr.org/country/costa-rica/
Cuba:	https://abortion-policies.srhr.org/country/cuba/
Dominican Republic:	www.hrw.org/report/2018/11/19/its-your-decision-its-your-life/total-criminalization-abortion-domin ican-republic

	https://abortion-policies.srhr.org/country/domin ican-republic/
Ecuador:	www.hrw.org/news/2019/04/25/ecuador-memoran dum-abortion-and-international-human-rights-law www.bbc.com/news/world-latin-america-49739495
El Salvador:	http://cpbucket.fiu.edu/1171-fiu01-wst-3015-secrvc-15022%2Fmod03_cfrr-criminalization_a bortion_elsalvador.pdf www.amnestyusa.org/what-el-salvadors-total-abor tion-ban-means-for-women-and-girls/
Guatemala:	https://reproductiverights.org/worldabortionlaws? country=GTM
Honduras:	www.hrw.org/news/2019/06/06/life-or-death-choices-women-living-under-honduras-abortion-ban https://reproductiverights.org/worldabortionlaws? country=GTM
Mexico:	https://abortion-policies.srhr.org/country/mexico/ https://reproductiverights.org/worldabortionlaws? country=MEX&category[295]=295
Nicaragua:	www.amnestyusa.org/pdfs/amr430012009en.pdf www.hrw.org/news/2017/07/31/nicaragua-abor tion-ban-threatens-health-and-lives
Panama:	www.unfpa.org/sites/default/files/resource-pdf/ FINAL_Panama.pdf www.worldpoliticsreview.com/articles/25711/ from-argentina-to-el-salvador-restrictive-abortion-laws-are-a-public-health-crisis
Paraguay=	http://resurj.org/post/abortion-paraguay https://reproductiverights.org/worldabortionlaws? country=PRY&category[295]=295
Uruguay=	www.mjilonline.org/uruguays-legalized-abortion-in-context/ www.mjilonline.org/uruguays-legalized-abortion-in-context/
Venezuela =	www.revistaamazonas.com/2018/12/17/las-comadres-purpuras/ https://avesawordpress.wordpress.com/2019/10/19/ es-legal-el-aborto-en-venezuela-marco-legal-nacio nal-e-internacional-en-materia-de-aborto/

Bibliography

Adrián, Tamara. 2020. Entrevista con Tamara Adrián, primera diputada transgénero de Venezuela. *GlobalVoices*, June 24.

Almeida, Guilherme. 2012. 'Homens Trans': Novos Matizes na Aquarela das Masculinidades? *Revista Estudos Feministas* 20(2): 513–523.

Almendral, Aurora and Danielle Villasana. 2021. What's next for these transgender asylum seekers stranded in Mexico? *National Geographic*.

Altman, Dennis. 1999. Globalization, Political Economy, and HIV/AIDS. *Theory and Society* 28(4): 559–584.

Amnesty International. 2017. No Safe Place. Report. Amnesty International.

Arenas, Reinaldo. 1992. *Antes que anochezca*. Barcelona, Tusquets Editores S.A.

Arrubia, Eduardo J. 2019. The Human Right to Gender Identity: From the International Human Rights Scenario to Latin American Domestic Legislation. *International Journal of Law, Policy and the Family* 33(3): 360–379.

Aultman, B. 2014. Cisgender. *TSQ: Transgender Studies Quarterly* 1(1–2): 61–62.

AVERT. 2019, 10 October. Transgender People, HIV and AIDS. www.avert.org/professionals/hiv-social-issues/key-affected-populations/transgender#fsootnote 29_tq12tz4.

Ayoub, Phillip M. and Douglas Page. 2020. When Do Opponents of Gay Rights Mobilize? Explaining Political Participation in Times of Backlash against Liberalism. *Political Research Quarterly* 73(3): 696–713.

Badgett, M. V. Lee, Sheila Nezhad, Kees Waaldijk and Yana van der Meulen Rodgers. 2014. The Relationship between LGBT Inclusion and Economic Development: An Analysis of Emerging Economies. Los Angeles: The Williams Institute, University of California Los Angeles School of Law.

Badgett, M. V. Lee, Kees Waaldijk and Yana van der Meulen Rodgers. 2019. The Relationship between LGBT Inclusion and Economic Development: Macro-Level Evidence. *Science Direct*.

Basabe-Serrano, Santiago. 2014. Some Determinants of Internal Judicial Independence: A Comparative Study of the Courts in Chile, Peru and Ecuador. *International Journal of Law, Crime and Justice* 42(2): 130–145.

Bellucci, Mabel. 2020. Entrevista por Dolores Curia: "De los gays aprendí a relacionarme amorosamente: cero cortejo." *Página 12*.

Ben, Pablo. 2004. Latin America: Colonial. In *glbtq: An Encyclopedia of Gay, Lesbian, Bisexual, Transgender, and Queer Culture*. C. J. Summers (ed.). www.glbtqarchive.com/sshindex.html

Ben, Pablo and Santiago Joaquin Insausti. 2017. Dictatorial Rule and Sexual Politics in Argentina: The Case of the Frente de Liberación Homosexual, 1967–1976. *Hispanic American Historical Review* 97(2): 297–325.

Biroli, Flávia and Mariana Caminotti. 2020. The Conservative Backlash against Gender in Latin America. *Politics & Gender* 16(1): 1–6.

Bleir, Garet and Kyle Andrew Smith. 2019. Fleeing to Survive: The Long Journey of LGBT Members of the Migrant Caravan. *Toward Freedom*, February 15.

Boas, Taylor C. 2021. Expanding the Public Square: Evangelicals and Electoral Politics in Latin America. In *The Inclusionary Turn in Contemporary Latin America*. Diana Kapiszewski, Steven Levitsky and Deborah J. Yashar, (eds.). New York: Cambridge University Press, 362–398.

Brown, Stephen. 2002. "Con discriminación y represión no hay democracia": The Lesbian and Gay Movement in Argentina. *Latin American Perspectives* 29(2): 119–138.

Bueno-Hansen, Pascha. 2017. The Emerging LGBTI Rights Challenge to Transitional Justice in Latin America. *International Journal of Transitional Justice* 12(1): 126–145.

Buriticá López, Isabel Cristina. 2013. Travesti: la construcción de la identidad individual y colectiva desde el cuerpo y el ejercicio de la prostitución. *La manzana de la discordia* 8(2): 71–86.

Bustos Rubio, Miguel and Demelsa Benito Sánchez. 2020. La aporofobia como agravante penal de discriminación. *Agenda Pública/El País*, July 4.

Cabezas, Amalia L. 2019. Latin American and Caribbean Sex Workers: Gains and Challenges in the Movement. *Anti-Trafficking Review* 12: 37–56.

Campana, Maximiliano and Juan Marco Vaggione. 2021. Courts and Same-Sex Marriage in Latin America. *Oxford Research Encyclopedias: Politics*.

Cardona Acuña, Luz Angela. 2019. Sotavento y Barlovento: El impacto de las interacciones societales y socio-estatales sobre los cambios legales relativos a la diversidad sexual en Perú y Ecuador (1980–2018). Social Sciences, Sociology, PhD dissertation, FLACSO México.

Carvalho, Mario and Sergio Carrara. 2013. Em Direção a Um Futuro Trans? Contribuição para a História do Movimento de Travestis e Transexuais no Brasil. *Sexualidad, Salud y Sociedad – Revista Latinoamericana* 14: 319–351.

CBMW (Council on Biblical Manhood and Womanhood). 2017. Nashville Statement. https://cbmw.org/nashville-statement/.

Center for Reproductive Rights. 2020. The World's Abortion Laws. www.reproductiverights.org/worldabortionlaws#law-policy-guide.

Chaux, Enrique, Manuela León, Lina Cuellar and Juliana Martínez. 2021. Public Opinion toward LGBT People and Rights in Latin America and the Caribbean. *Oxford Research Encyclopedia*.

Chávez, Daniel Brittany. 2016. Transmaculine Insurgency: Masculinity and Dissidence in Feminist Movements in México. *TSQ: Transgender Studies Quarterly* 3(1–2): 58–64.

Choi, Soon Kyu, Shahrzad Divsalar, Jennifer Flórez-Donado, Krystal Kittle, Ilan H. Meyer and Prince Torres-Salaza. 2020. *Stress, Health, and Well-being of LGBT People in Colombia: Results from A National Survey.* Los Angeles and Bogota: The Williams Institute and the Colombia Collaborative Project.

Corrales, Javier. 2017. Understanding the Uneven Spread of LGBT rights in Latin America and the Caribbean, 1999–2013. *Journal of Research in Gender Studies* 7: 52–82.

Corrales, Javier. 2018. How Argentina Has Made Halting Progress on Abortion Rights. *The New York Times*, August 10. www.nytimes.com/2018/08/10/opinion/how-argentina-has-made-halting-progress-on-abortion-rights.html.

Corrales, Javier. 2020a. The Expansion of LGBT Rights in Latin America and the Backlash. In *The Oxford Handbook of Global LGBT and Sexual Diversity Politics.* Michael J. Bosia, Sandra M. McEvoy and Momin Rahman (eds.), New York: Oxford University Press, 185–200: 185–200.

Corrales, Javier. 2020b. The 2020 Top Ten LGBT Stories from Latin America and the Caribbean. Global Americans, December 28. https://theglobalamericans.org/2020/12/the-2020-top-ten-lgbt-stories-from-latin-america-and-the-caribbean/.

Corrales, Javier and Mario Pecheny. 2010. Introduction. In *The Politics of Sexuality in Latin America.* Javier Corrales and Mario Pecheny (eds.). Pittsburgh, PA: Pittsburgh University Press, 1–30.

Corrales, Javier and Iñaki Sagarzazu. 2019. Not all 'Sins' Are Rejected Equally: Resistance to LGBT Rights across Religions in Colombia. *Politics and Religion* 13(2): 351–377.

Cossette, Laura and Kenia Saba Perez. 2019. The Fear of the "Gender Ideology": Erasing Sexual and Gender Minorities from the Colombian Peace Process. Accessed May 29, 2020, www.lawg.org/the-fear-of-the-gender-ideology-erasing-sexual-and-gender-minorities-from-the-colombian-peace-process/.

Crahan, Margaret E. 1989. Catholicism in Cuba. *Cuban Studies* 19: 3–24.

Crehan, Phil, Liam Rezende, John Wolf, Peter Jordan and Ceren Altincekic. 2021. *The Economic Case for LGBT+ Inclusion in the Caribbean.* London: Open for Business.

Curiel, Ochy. 2013. *La nación heterosexual. Análisis del discurso jurídico y el régimen heterosexual desde la antropología de la dominación.* Bogota: Brecha Lésbica.

Curiel, Ochy, Sabine Masson and Jules Falquet. 2005. Féminismes dissidents en Amérique latine et aux Caraïbes. *Nouvelles Questions Féministes* 24(2): 4–13.

Daby, Mariela and Mason Moseley. 2021. Feminist Mobilization and the Abortion Debate in Latin America: Lessons from Argentina. *Politics & Gender*, 1–35.

Daich, Deborah. 2012. ¿Abolicionismo o reglamentarismo? Aportes de la antropología feminista para el debate local sobre la prostitución. *Runa* 23 (1): 71–84.

Daudelin, Jean and W. E. Hewitt. 1995. Churches and Politics in Latin America: Catholicism at the Crossroads. *Third World Quarterly* 16(2): 221–236.

de Abreu Maia, Lucas, Albert Chiu and Scott Desposato. 2020. LGBT Civil Rights Do Not Provoke Backlash: Evidence from Latin America. *SSRN Social Science Research Network*.

De Jesus, Jaqueline Gomes and Hailey Alves. 2012. Feminismo Transgênero e Movimentos de Mulheres Transexuais. *Revista Cronos* 11(2): 8–19.

de la Dehesa, Rafael. 2010. *Queering the Public Sphere in Mexico and Brazil: Sexual Rights Movements in Emerging Democracies*. Durham, NC: Duke University Press.

DW (*Deutsche Welle*). 2020. "Visibilidad lésbica: 'El lesbofeminismo llegó para quedarse.'" *DW América Latina*, April 22.

Díez, Jordi. 2015. *The Politics of Gay Marriage in Latin America: Argentina, Chile, and Mexico*. New York: Cambridge University Press.

Díez, Jordi and Michelle L. Dion. 2018. New Media and Support for Same-Sex Marriage. *Latin American Research Review* 53(3): 466–484.

Dion, Michelle L. and Jordi Díez. 2017. Democratic values, religiosity, and support for same-sex marriage in Latin America. *Latin American Politics and Society* 59(4): 75–98.

Dion, Michelle L. and Jordi Díez. 2020. Social Contact with Same-Sex Married Couples and Support for Marriage Equality: Evidence from Argentina. *Politics, Groups, and Identities*, 1–19.

Dixon, Kwame. 2020. Afro-Latin Social Movements in Latin America and the Caribbean. *Oxford Research Encyclopedia, Politics*. Oxford: Oxford University Press.

Domínguez-Ruvalcaba, Héctor. 2016. *Translating the Queer: Body Politics and Transnational Conversations*. London: Zed Books.

Duarte Bastian, Ángela Ixkic. 2012. From the Margins of Latin American Feminism: Indigenous and Lesbian Feminisms. *Signs: Journal of Women in Culture and Society* 38(1): 153–178.

ECLAC. 2020. Femicide or Feminicide. https://oig.cepal.org/en/indicators/femicide-or-feminicide.

Encarnación, Omar. G. 2011. Latin America's Gay Rights Revolution. *Journal of Democracy* 22(2): 104–118.

Encarnación, Omar. G. 2014. Why Latin American Courts Favor Gay Rights. *The New York Times*, January 29.

Encarnación, Omar. G. 2015. *Out in the Periphery*. New York: Oxford University Press.

Encarnación, Omar G. 2018. A Latin American Puzzle: Gay Rights Landscapes in Argentina and Brazil. *Human Rights Quarterly* 40(1): 194–218.

Encuentro Lésbico Feminista de Abya Yala. 2016. Memoria: X Encuentro Lésbico Feminista de Abya Yala del 9 al 14 de octubre Chnauta-Colombia.

Faber, Tom. 2018. Welcome to Jamaica – No Longer "the Most Homophobic Place on Earth." *The Guardian*, December 6.

Facchini, Regina. 2003. Movimento Homossexual no Brasil: Recompondo um histórico. *Cad. AEL, Universidad Estadual de Campinas, Instituto de Filosofia e Ciências Humanas, Arquivo Edgar Leuenroth* 10(18/19).

Facchini, Regina and Isadora Lins França. 2013. On Hues, Tints and Shades: Subjects, Connections and Challenges in the Brazilian LGBT Movement. In *Sexuality, Culture and Politics: A South American Reader*. S. C. Horácio Sívori, Jane Russo et. al. (eds.). Rio de Janeiro: CEPESC, 89–108: 82–123.

Fassin, Éric. 2020. Anti-Gender Campaigns, Populism, and Neoliberalism in Europe and Latin America. *LASA Forum* 51(2): 67–71.

Faur, Eleonor and Mara Viveros Vigoya. 2020. La ofensiva conservadora contra la "ideología de género" y sus estrategias de avanzada en América Latina. *LASA Forum* 51(2): 11–16.

Fernández Anderson, Cora. 2018. In Argentina, Feminists versus the Catholic Church. *NACLA Report on the Americas*, June 7.

Fernández Anderson, Cora. 2020. *Fighting for Abortion Rights in Latin America: Social Movements, State Allies and Institutions*. New York: Taylor & Francis.

Figari, Carlos. 2010. El movimiento LGBT en América Latina: institucionalizaciones oblicuas. In *Movilizaciones, protestas e identidades colectivas en la Argentina del bicentenario*. Astor Massetti, Ernesto Villanueva and Marcelo Gómez, (eds.), Buenos Aires: Nueva Trilce, 225–240.

Frasca, Tim. 2005. *AIDS in Latin America*. London: Palgrave MacMillan.

Friedman, Elisabeth Jay. 2009. Gender, Sexuality and the Latin American Left: Testing the Transformation. *Third World Quarterly* 30(2): 415–433.

Friedman, Elisabeth Jay. 2012. Constructing "The Same Rights with the Same Names": The Impact of Spanish Norm Diffusion on Marriage Equality in Argentina. *Latin American Politics and Society* 54(4): 29–59.

Friedman, Elisabeth Jay and Constanza Tabbush. 2019. Introduction. In *Seeking Rights from the Left: Gender, Sexuality and the Latin American Pink Tide*. Elisabeth Jay Friedman (ed.). Durham, NC: Duke University Press, 1–47.

Gamson, Joshua. 1995. Must Identity Movements Self-Destruct? A Queer Dilemma. *Social Problems* 42(3): 390–407.

Garrard, Virginia. 2019. Dissenting Religion: Protestantism in Latin America. In *The Oxford History of Protestant Dissenting Traditions, Vol. IV: The Twentieth Century: Traditions in a Global Context.* Jehu J. Hanciles (ed.). New York: Oxford University Press, 359–383.

Garriga-López, Claudia Sofía. 2016. Transfeminist Crossroads: Reimagining the Ecuadorian State. *TSQ: Transgender Studies Quarterly* 3(1–2): 104–119.

Garriga-López, Claudia Sofía. 2019. Transfeminism. In *Global Encylopedia of Lesbian, Gay, Bisexual, Transgender and Queer (LGBTQ) History.* Howard Chiang, Anjali Arondekar, Marc Epprecht et al. (eds.). Farmington Hills, MI: Charles Scribner's Sons, 1619–1622.

Garza, Rebeca. 2018. *Trans*: entre lo personal y lo político: violencias de género y participación política electoral de las personas trans* en México 1990–2016 dentro del sistema electoral mexicano.* www.academia.edu/39330925/ TRANS_ENTRE_LO_PERSONAL_Y_LO_POL%C3%8DTICO_Violencias _de_g%C3%A9nero_y_participaci%C3%B3n_pol%C3%ADtica_electoral_de _las_personas_trans_en_M%C3%A9xico_1990_2016_dentro_del_sistema_ele ctoral_mexicano_Rebeca_Garza.

Gomez, Eduardo J. 2010. Friendly Government, Cruel Society: AIDS and the Politics of Homosexual Strategic Mobilization in Brazil. In *The Politics of Sexuality in Latin America.* Javier Corrales and Mario Pecheny (eds.). Pittsburgh, PA: Pittsburgh University Press, 223–250.

Gonzalez-Rostani, Valentina, Scott Morgenstern and Marika Olijar. 2020. Latin American Legislators Support for Same-Sex Marriage. Evidence from the PELA-USAL Database.

González, María Virginia. 2013. Una aproximación a la construcción de la alteridad "negra" y a los debates instaurados por las afrodescendientes en el feminismo latinoamericano. *Anuario de la Facultad de Ciencias Humanas* 10(2): 1–12.

Green, James N. 2012. "Who Is the Macho Who Wants to Kill Me?": Male Homosexuality, Revolutionary Masculinity, and the Brazilian Armed Struggle of the 1960s and 70s. *Hispanic American Historical Review* 92(3): 437–469.

Green, James N. 2019. The LGBTT Movement, the Brazilian Left, and the Process of Democratization. In *The Brazilian Left in the 21st Century: Conflict and Conciliation in Peripheral Capitalism.* Vladimir Puzone and Luis Felipe Miguel (eds.). London: Palgrave Macmillan, 183–204.

Grey, Cornel and Nikoli Attai. 2020. LGBT Rights, Sexual Citizenship, and Blacklighting in the Anglophone Caribbean: What Do Queers Want, What

Does Colonialism Need? In *The Oxford Handbook of Global LGBT and Sexual Diversity Politics*. Michael J. Bosia, Sandra M. McEvoy and Momin Rahman (eds.). New York: Oxford University Press, 249–266.

Guy, Donna J. 2010. Gender and Sexuality in Latin America. In *The Oxford Handbook of Latin American History*. Jose C. Moya (ed.). New York: Oxford University Press, 367–375.

Hagopian, Frances. 2008. Latin American Catholicism in an Age of Religious and Political Pluralism: A Framework for Analysis. *Comparative Politics* 40(2): 149–168.

Halliday, Terence C. and Gregory Shaffer. 2015. Transnational Legal Orders. In *Transnational Legal Orders*. Terence C. Halliday and Gregory Shaffer (eds.). New York: Cambridge University Press, 3–72.

Holbrook, Joseph. 2010. The Catholic Church in Cuba, 1959–1962: The Clash of Ideologies. *International Journal of Cuban Studies* 2(3/4): 264–275.

Hunter, Wendy and Timothy J. Power. 2019. Bolsonaro and Brazil's Illiberal Backlash. *Journal of Democracy* 30(1): 68–82.

Htun, Mala. 2003. *Sex and the State: Abortion, Divorce, and the Family Under Latin American Dictatorships and Democracies.*. New York: Cambridge University Press.

Htun, Mala. 2009. Life, Liberty, and Family Values: Church and State in the Struggle Over Abortion in Latin America. In *Religious Pluralism, and the Catholic Church in in Latin America*. Frances Hagopian (ed.). Notre Dame, IN: University of Notre Dame Press, 335–364.

ILGA World: Lucas Ramon Mendos. December 2019. State-Sponsored Homophobia 2019: Global Legislation Overview Update. December 10.

ILGA World : Lucas Ramon Mendos. 2020. Curbing Deception: A World Survey on Legal Regulation of So-Called "Conversion Therapies." Geneva: ILGA World.

International Human Rights Law Clinic. 2012. *Sexual Diversity in El Salvador: A Report on the Human Rights Situation of the LGBT Community*. Berkeley: University of California, Berkeley.

Iricibar, Valen. 2019. Trans Exclusion Bid Underlines Growing Pains of Feminist Movement. *Buenos Aires Times*, March 9.

J. E.W., Jr. 1966. Editorial: Church and State in Latin America. *Journal of Church and State* 8(2): 173–185.

Jackman, Mahalia. 2017. Protecting the Fabric of Society? Heterosexual Views on the Usefulness of the Anti-Gay Laws in Barbados, Guyana and Trinidad and Tobago. *Culture, Health & Sexuality* 19(1): 91–106.

Johnson, Richard Greggory, Sean McCandless and Hugo Renderos. 2020. An Exploratory Study of Transgender Inmate Populations in Latin America. *Public Integrity* 22(4): 330–343.

Joseph, Janice. 2017. Victims of Femicide in Latin America: Legal and Criminal Justice Responses. *Temida* 20(1): 3–21.

Kaas, Hailey. 2016. Birth of Transfeminism in Brazil. *TSQ: Transgender Studies Quarterly* 3(1–2): 145–149.

Kane, Gillian. 2008. Abortion Law Reform in Latin America: Lessons for Advocacy. *Gender and Development* 16(2): 361–375.

Kapur, Ratna. 2018. There's a Problem with the LGBT Rights Movement – It's Limiting Freedom. *The Conversation*, September 17.

Kirk, Emily J. and Robert Huish. 2018. Transsexuals' Right to Health? A Cuban Case Study. *Health and Human Rights* 20(2): 215–222.

Kollman, Kelly and Iñaki Sagarzazu. 2017. LGBTI Rights Expansion in the Global South: Explaining the Diffusion of Same-Sex Unions Policy in Latin America. *Paper presented at the MPSA meeting*. Chicago, IL, April 6–9.

Kosciw, Joseph G. and Adrian Zongrone. 2019. *A Global School Climate Crisis: Insights on Lesbian, Gay, Bisexual,Transgender & Queer Students in Latin America*. New York: GLSEN.

La Fountain-Stokes, Lawrence. 2004. De sexilio(s) y diáspora(s) homosexual-(es) latina(s): El caso de la cultura puertorriqueña y nuyorican 'queer.' *Debate Feminista*(29): 138–157.

Latinobarómetro. 2014. Las religiones en tiempos del Papa Francisco. April 16, Santiago, Chile.

Lecuona, Laura. 2020. México, el Parlamento de Mujeres, el lobby trans y los derechos de las mujeres basados en el sexo. *Tribuna Feminista*, August 10.

Leiner, Marvin. 1994. *Sexual Politics in Cuba: Machismo, Homosexuality, and AIDS*. Boulder, CO: Westview Press.

Lester, Toni. 2012. Machismo at the Crossroads: Recent Developments in Costa Rican Gay Rights Law. *Michigan State International Law Review* 20(2): 421.

Longaker, Jacob R. and Donald P. Haider-Markel. 2014. Transgender Policy in Latin American Countries An Overview and Comparative Perspective on Framing. In *Transgender Rights and Politics*. D. P. Haider-Markel and J. K. Taylor (eds.). Ann Arbor: University of Michigan Press, 49–80.

López, Jairo Antonio. 2017. Los derechos LGBT en México: Acción colectiva a nivel subnacional. *European Review of Latin American and Caribbean Studies* 104: 69–88.

López, Jairo Antonio. 2018. Movilización y contramovilización frente a los derechos LGBTI. Respuestas conservadoras al reconocimiento de los derechos humanos. *Estudios sociológicos* 36: 161–187.

Lopez, Oscar. 2018. Fleeing Persecution, LGBT+ Migrants Seek Refuge in South America. *Reuters*, December 19.

Lowy, Michael and Claudia Pompan. 1993. Marxism and Christianity in Latin America. *Latin American Perspectives* 20(4): 28–42.

Lumsden, Ian. 1996. *Machos, Maricones and Gays: Cuba and Homosexuality.* Philadelphia, PA: Temple University Press.

Malamud, Carlos. 2018. The Political Expansion of Evangelical Churches in Latin America. Madrid: Instituto Real Elcano, December 12.

Malta, Monica, Reynaldo Cardoso, Luiz Montenegro et al. 2019. Sexual and Gender Minorities Rights in Latin America and the Caribbean: A Multi-Country Evaluation. *BMC International Health and Human Rights* 19(1): 31–31.

Marcus-Delgado, Jane. 2020. *The Politics of Abortion in Latin America: Public Debates, Private Lives*. Boulder, CO: Lynne Rienner.

Marsiaj, Juan. 2006. Social Movements and Political Parties: Gays, Lesbians and Travestis and the Struggle for Inclusion in Brazil. *Canadian Journal of Latin American and Caribbean Studies* 31(62): 167–196.

Martinez-Reyes, Consuelo. 2018. *Hispanic Caribbean Sexiles*, Oxford: Oxford University Press.

Mascarenhas Neto, Rubens and Vinícious Zanoli. 2019. Black, LGBT and from the Favelas: An Ethnographic Account on Disidentificatory Performances of an Activist Group in Brazil. *Culture Unbound: Journal of Current Cultural Research* 11(1): 124–140.

Mathema, Silva. 2018. They Are (Still) Refugees: People Continue to Flee Violence in Latin American Countries. Washington, DC: Center for American Progress, June 1.

Matos, Marlise. 2019. Gender and Sexuality in Brazilian Public Policy: Progress and Regression in Depatriarchalizing and Deheteronormalizing the State. In *Seeking Rights from the Left: Gender, Sexuality and the Latin American Pink Tide*. Elisabeth Jay Friedman (ed.). Durham, NC, Duke University Press, 144–172.

McGee, Marcus J. and Karen Kampwirth. 2015. The Co-optation of LGBT Movements in Mexico and Nicaragua: Modernizing Clientelism? *Latin American Politics and Society* 57(4): 51–73.

Mejores Empleos. 2019. #TransLaboral: la discriminación laboral de la comunidad trans. *Mejores Empleos: La revista del mundo laboral.*

Merentes, José Ramón. 2010. Gay Rights in Venezuela under Hugo Chávez, 1999–2009. In *The Politics of Sexuality in Latin America*. Javier Corrales and Mario Pecheny (eds.). Pittsburgh, PA: University of Pittsburgh Press, 220–223.

Mogrovejo, Norma. 1996. *El amor es b x h/2: una propuesta de análisis histórico-metodológica del movimiento lésbico y sus amores con los movimientos homosexual y feminista en América Latina.* Mexico City: Centro de Documentación y Archivo Histórico Lésbico.

Mogrovejo, Norma. 2000. *Un amor que se atrevió a decir su nombre: La lucha de las lesbianas y su relación con los movimientos homosexuales y feministas de América Latina.* Mexico City: Centro de Documentación y Archivo Histórico Lésbico.

Mogrovejo, Norma. 2018. *Del Sexilio al Matrimonio: Ciudadanía sexual en la era del consumo neoliberal,* 3rd ed. Bilbao: DDT Liburuak.

Molyneux, Maxine. 2017. The Battle over 'Gender Ideology'. *International Politics and Society.* December 8. www.ips-journal.eu/regions/latin-america/the-battle-over-gender-ideology-2472/

Morad, Moshe. 2008. 'Invertidos' in Afro-Cuban Religion. *The Gay and Lesbian Review*: 26–28.

Morcillo, Santiago and Karina Felitti. 2017. 'Mi cuerpo es mío'. Debates y disputas de los feminismos argentinos en torno al aborto y al sexo comercial, *Amerika* [On line], July 1.

Morgan, Lynn M. 2014. Claiming Rosa Parks: Conservative Catholic Bids for 'Rights' in Contemporary Latin America. *Culture, Health & Sexuality* 16 (10): 1245–1259.

Morgan, Lynn M. 2015. Reproductive Rights or Reproductive Justice? Lessons from Argentina. *Health and Human Rights* 17(1): 136–147.

Muñoz-Pogossian, Betilde. 2020. Democracia y derechos de las personas LGBTI en América Latina: reformas para garantizar el derecho a la identidad y el derecho al voto de las personas trans, 2012–2020. *Revista Derecho Electoral*(20): 87–109.

Murray, Laura R., Jonathan Garcia, Miguel Muñoz-Laboy and Richard G. Parker. 2011. Strange Bedfellows: The Catholic Church and Brazilian National AIDS Program in the Response to HIV/AIDS in Brazil. *Social Science & Medicine* 72(6): 945–952.

Murray, Stephen O. 1995a. Homosexual Categorization in Cross-Cultural Context. In *Latin American Male Homosexualities*. Stephen O. Murray (ed.). Albuquerque: University of New Mexico Press.

Murray, Stephen O. 1995b. Machismo, Male Homosexuality and Latino Culture. *Latin American Male Homosexualities*. Stephen O. Murray (ed.). Albuquerque: University of New Mexico Press.

Navarro, María Camila, Jaime Barrientos, Fabiola Gómez and Joaquín Bahamondes. 2019. Tolerance of Homosexuality in South American Countries: A Multilevel Analysis of Related Individual and

Sociocultural Factors. *International Journal of Sexual Health* 31(3): 257–268.

Neel, Robert. 2016. Stretching Hearts: Understanding Sexuality Politics and Institutional Homophobia in the Anglo-Caribbean. Bachelor Thesis in Political Science. Amherst, MA, Amherst College.

Nesvig, Martin. 2001. The Complicated Terrain of Latin American Homosexuality. *Hispanic American Historical Review* 81(3–4).

Pecheny, Mario. 2010. Sociability, Secrets, and Identities: Key Issues in Sexual Politics in Latin America. In *The Politics of Sexuality in Latin America*. Javier Corrales and Mario Pecheny (eds.). Pittsburgh, PA: University of Pittsburgh Press.

Pérez Díaz, Vanessa. 2019. La comunidad Lgbt movió el año pasado US$253.000 millones en América Latina. *La República* (Colombia).

Pérez Guadalupe, José Luis and Sebastian Grundberger. 2017. *Between God and Emperor: On the Political Influence of Evangelical Churches in Latin America*. Konrad-Adenauer-Stiftung, December 22.

Pew Research Center. 2014. Religion in Latin America: Widespread Change in a Historically Catholic Region. Pew Research Center.

Picq, Manuela. 2018. *Vernacular Sovereignties*. Tucson: University of Arizona Press.

Pierceson, Jason. 2013. Variations in the Judicialization of Same-Sex Marriage Politics in Latin America. In *Same-Sex Marriage in Latin America: Promise and Resistance*. Jason Pierceson, Adriana Piatta-Crocker and Shawn Schulenberg (eds.). Plymouth, UK: Lexington Books, 53–69.

Piscitelli, Adriana. 2014. Transnational Sisterhood? Brazilian Feminisms Facing Prostitution. *Latin American Policy* 5(2): 221–235.

Poushter, Jacob and Nicholas O. Kent. 2020. The Global Divide on Homosexuality Persists. Pew Research Center, June 25.

Prieur, Annick. 1998. *Mema's House, Mexico City: On Transvestites, Queens and Machos*. Chicago: University of Chicago Press.

Rahman, Momin. 2000. *Sexuality and Democracy: Identities and Strategies in Lesbian and Gay Politics*. Edinburgh: Edinburgh University Press.

Ramos, Deysi. 2015. Así nació el movimiento gay en Venezuela. Sin Etiquetas: Plataforma Digital. February 9. http://sinetiquetas.org/2015/02/09/asi-nacio-el-movimiento-gay-en-venezuela/.

Ratzinger, Joseph Cardinal. 1986. Letter to the Bishops of the Catholic Church on the Pastoral Care of Homosexual Persons, Vatican, Congregation for the Doctrine of the Faith.

RedLacTrans. 2018. Violaciones a los Derechos Humanos de Mujeres Trans en Costa Rica, El Salvador, Guatemala, Honduras y Panama.

RedLacTrans. 2018. Waiting to Die: Regional Report 2016–2017.

RedLacTrans. 2019. Plan estratégico 2019–2023: Incidencia política.

Reis Brandão, Elaine and Cristiane da Silva Cabral. 2019. Sexual and Reproductive Rights Under Attack: The Advance of Political and Moral Conservatism in Brazil. *Sexual and Reproductive Health Matters* 27(2): 76–86.

Reynolds, Andrew. 2020. Queer Politics: LGBT Members of Parliament in Total (National Assembly), 1976–2020. Unpublished paper, University of North Carolina at Chapel Hill. www.queerpolitics.org/.

Richardson, Diane. 2017. Rethinking Sexual Citizenship. *Sociology* 51(2): 208–224.

Rios, Roger Raupp. 2018. Por um direito democrático da sexualidade. In *Direitos sexuais e direito de família em perspectiva queer*. Daniel Borrillo, Fernando Seffner and Roger Raupp Rios (eds.). Porto Alegre: Editora da UFCSPA (Universidade Federal de Ciências da Saúde de Porto Alegre), 79–117.

Rodríguez-Rondón, Manuel Alejandro and Claudia Rivera-Amarillo. 2020. Producción de conocimiento y activismo antigénero en América Latina. *LASA Forum* 51(2).

Schulenberg, Shawn. 2013. Lavender Tide? LGBT Rights and the Latin American Left Today. In *Same-Sex Marriage in Latin America: Promise and Resistance*. Jason Pierceson, Adriana Piatta-Crocker and Shawn Schulenberg (eds.). Plymouth, UK: Lexington Books: 23–39.

Serrano-Amaya, José Fernando. 2018. *Homophobic Violence in Armed Conflict and Political Transition*. New York: Palgrave Macmillan.

Simonetto, Patricio. 2017. Movimientos de liberación homosexual en América Latina. Aportes historiográficos desde una perspectiva comparada entre Argentina, Brasil, Chile, Colombia y México (1967–1982). *Iberoamericana* 17(65): 157–177.

Singh, Susheela, Lisa Remez, Gilda Sedgh, Lorraine Kwok and Tsuyoshi Onda. 2018. *Abortion Worldwide 2017: Uneven Progress and Unequal Access*. New York: Guttmacher Institute.

Smallman, Shawn C. 2007. *The AIDS Pandemic in Latin America*. Chapel Hill: University of North Carolina Press.

Smith, Amy Erica. 2019. *Religion and Brazilian Democracy: Mobilizing the People of God*. Cambridge, UK, and New York: Cambridge University Press.

Smith, Amy Erica and Taylor C. Boas. 2020. Religion, Sexuality Politics, and the Transformation of Latin American Electorates. Paper prepared for APSA.

Somma, Nicolás M., Matías A. Bargsted and Eduardo Valenzuela. 2017. Mapping Religious Change in Latin America. *Latin American Politics and Society* 59(1): 119–142.

Somma, Nicolás M., Federico M. Rossi and Sofía Donoso. 2019. The Attachment of Demonstrators to Institutional Politics: Comparing LGBTIQ Pride Marches in Argentina and Chile. *Bulletin of Latin American Research* 39(3): 380–397.

Stepan, Alfred C. 2000. Religion, Democracy, and the "Twin Tolerations." *Journal of Democracy* 11(4): 37–57.

Su, Yvonne and Tyler Valiquette. 2020. More Protection Urgently Needed for Venezuelan LGBTQ+ Refugees in Brazil. *The Conversation*, February 3, https://theconversation.com/more-protection-urgently-needed-for-venezuelan-lgbtq-refugees-in-brazil-129040.

Summers, Claude J. 2004. Roman Catholicism. In *glbtq: An Encyclopedia of Gay, Lesbian, Bisexual, Transgender, and Queer Culture* C. J. Summers (ed.). www.glbtqarchive.com/sshindex.html.

Symons, Jonathan and Dennis Altman. 2015. International Norm Polarization: Sexuality as a Subject of Human Rights Protection. *International Theory* 7(1): 61–95.

Télam. 2020. Un panorama federal sobre identidad de género, a 8 años de la sanción de la ley en Argentina. *Télam*, August 5.

Thayer, Millie. 1997. Identity, Revolution, and Democracy: Lesbian Movements in Central America. *Social Problems* 44(3): 386–407.

Torres-Ruiz, Antonio. 2011. HIV/AIDS and Sexual Minorities in Mexico: A Globalized Struggle for the Protection of Human Rights. *Latin American Research Review* 46(1): 30–53.

Trans Murder Monitor. 2019. TMM Update Trans Day of Remembrance 2019.

UNAIDS. 2014. The Gap Report. Joint United Nations Programme on HIV/AIDS (UNAIDS). http://files.unaids.org/en/media/unaids/contentassets/documents/unaidspublication/2014/UNAIDS_Gap_report_en.pdf, UNAIDS: Joint United Nations Programme on HIV/AIDS.

Vasconi, Tomás A., Elina Peraza Martell and Fred Murphy. 1993. Social Democracy and Latin America. *Latin American Perspectives* 20(1): 99–113.

Vatican City. 2019. 'Male and Female He Created Them': Towards a Path of Dialogue on the Question of Gender Theory in Education. Vatican City: Vatican Press.

Vela Barba, Estefanía. 2017. La verdadera ideología de género. *New York Times Edición Español*, July 11.

Velasco, Kristopher. 2019. A Growing Queer Divide: The Divergence between Transnational Advocacy Networks and Foreign Aid in Diffusing LGBT Policies. *International Studies Quarterly* 64(1): 120–132.

Velasco, Kristopher. 2020. Queering the World Society: Global Norms, Rival Transnational Networks, and the Contested Case of LGBT Rights. Queer Politics, Webinar.

Weeks, Jeffrey. 2007. *The World We Have Won*. London: Routledge.

Weiss, Meredith L. and Michael J. Bosia (eds.). 2013. *Global Homophobia: States, Movements and the Politics of Oppression*. Chicago: University of Illinois Press.

Wilets, Jim. 2010. Divergence between LGBTI Legal, Political, and Social Progress in the Caribbean and Latin America. In *The Politics of Sexuality in Latin America*. Javier Corrales and Mario Pecheny (eds.). Pittsburgh, PA: University of Pittsburgh Press, 349–357.

Winter, Sam, Milton Diamond, Jamison Green, Dan Karasic, Terry Reed, Stephen Whittle and Kevan Wylie. 2016. Transgender People: Health at the Margins of Society. *The Lancet* 388(10042): 390–400.

Wright, Timothy. 2000. Gay Organizations, NGOs, and the Globalization of Sexual Identity: The Case of Bolivia. *Journal of Latin American Anthropology* 5(2): 89–111.

Wood, Susan, Lilián Abracinskas, Sonia Correa and Mario Pecheny. 2016. Reform of Abortion Law in Uruguay: Context, Process and Lessons Learned. *Reproductive Health Matters* 24(48): 102–110.

Xie, Selena and Javer Corrales. 2010. LGBT Rights in Ecuador's 2008 Constitution: Victories and Setbacks. In *The Politics of Sexuality*. Javier Corrales and Mario Pecheny (eds.). Pittsburgh, PA: University of Pittsburgh Press, 224–229.

Youde, Jeremy. 2020. The Global HIV/AIDS and LGBT Movement. In *The Oxford Handbook of Global LGBT and Sexual Diversity Politics*. Michael J. Bosia, Sandra M. McEvoy and Momin Rahman (eds.). New York: Oxford University Press.

Zilla, Claudia. 2018. Evangelicals and Politics in Latin America. Berlin: German Institute for International and Security Affairs. SWP Comment No. 4646.

Acknowledgments

I am enormously grateful to the editors and anonymous reviews for their insightful comments and guidance. I am also grateful to a number of students who helped with various aspects of the research as part of their final project or as research assistants at Amherst College in the spring of 2020: Camila A. Blanco, Scott Brasesco, Se Yoon Choi, Sydney Ireland, Danielle R. King, Jack D. Kiryk, Jasper Lile, Kyabeth Rincón, and Erica P. Sanders. They were an inspiration.

Elements in the Series

Maria Victoria Murillo

Columbia University

Maria Victoria Murillo is Professor of Political Science and International Affairs at Columbia University. She is the author of *Political Competition, Partisanship, and Policymaking in the Reform of Latin American Public Utilities* (Cambridge, 2009). She is also editor of *Carreras Magisteriales, Desempeño Educativo y Sindicatos de Maestros en América Latina* (2003), and co-editor of *Argentine Democracy: the Politics of Institutional Weakness* (2005). She has published in edited volumes as well as in the *American Journal of Political Science, World Politics,* and *Comparative Political Studies,* among others.

Juan Pablo Luna

The Pontifical Catholic University of Chile

Juan Pablo Luna is Professor in the Department of Political Science at The Pontifical Catholic University of Chile. He is the author of *Segmented Representation; Political Party Strategies in Unequal Democracies,* and has co-authored *Latin American Party Systems* (Cambridge, 2010). His work on political representation, state capacity, and organized crime has appeared in *Comparative Political Studies, Revista de Ciencia Política,* the *Journal of Latin American Studies, Latin American Politics and Society, Studies in Comparative International Development,* among others.

Tulia G. Falleti

University of Pennsylvania

Tulia G. Falleti is the Class of 1965 Term Associate Professor of Political Science, Director of the Latin American and Latino Studies Program, and Senior Fellow of the Leonard Davis Institute for Health Economics at the University of Pennsylvania. She is the author of the award-winning *Decentralization and Subnational Politics in Latin America* (Cambridge, 2010). She is co-editor of *The Oxford Handbook of Historical Institutionalism,* among other edited books. Her articles have appeared in many edited volumes and journals such as the *American Political Science Review* and *Comparative Political Studies.*

Andrew Schrank

Brown University

Andrew Schrank is the Olive C. Watson Professor of Sociology and International & Public Affairs at Brown University. His articles on business, labor, and the state in Latin America have appeared in the *American Journal of Sociology, Comparative Politics, Comparative Political Studies, Latin American Politics & Society, Social Forces,* and *World Development,* among other journals, and his co-authored book, *Root-Cause Regulation: Labor Inspection in Europe and the Americas.*

Cambridge Elements ≡

Elements in the Series

Printed in the United States
by Baker & Taylor Publisher Services